Old-Fashioned Meatballs in Red Sauce *page 128*

Tomato, Basil, and Bread Soup *page 30*

Fresh Linguine with Butter, Parmesan Cheese, and Mushrooms *page 46*

Rice, Sweet Pepper, and Shrimp Soup *page 28*

Sautéed Bass with Fresh Tomatoes and Basil *page 92*

Quick Risotto with Tuna and Tomatoes *page 68*

Oven-Roasted Sea Scallops with Capers and White Wine *page 80*

Chicken Breasts with Pancetta and Sage *page 108*

Roast Chicken Legs with Balsamic Vinegar and Tomato *page 112*

Little New Potatoes with Lemon Zest *page 196*

Pot Roast with Red Wine, Italian Style *page 130*

Rosemary-Pepper Pizza Bread *page 10*

Arugula, Blood Orange, and Fennel Salad *page 154*

Fresh Ricotta with Fruit *page 220*

Figs with Orange and Basil *page 210*

Baked Spinach with Garlic Bread Crumbs *page 192*

The Simpler The Better

Sensational Italian Meals

THE SIMPLER THE BETTER

Sensational Home Cooking in 3 Easy Steps

Sensational Italian Meals

Sensational One-Dish Meals

The Simpler The Better

SENSATIONAL ITALIAN MEALS

LESLIE REVSIN

with Rick Rodgers

WILEY

JOHN WILEY & SONS, INC.

For general information on our other products and services, please contact our Customer Care Department within the United States at (800) 762-2974, outside the United States at (317) 572-3993 or fax (317) 572-4002.

Wiley also publishes its books in a variety of electronic formats. Some content that appears in print may not be available in electronic books. For more information about Wiley products, visit our web site at www.wiley.com.

Library of Congress Cataloging-in-Publication Data:
Revsin, Leslie.
The simpler the better : sensational Italian meals / by Leslie Revsin.
     p. cm.
  Includes index.
  ISBN 0-471-48232-3 (pbk.)
  1. Cookery, Italian. I. Title.

  TX723.R45 2005
  641.5945—dc22

                    2004029642

Book design by Richard Oriolo
Photography copyright © 2005 by Duane Winfield
Food styling by Megan Fawn Schlow
Prop styling by Duane Winfield and Justin Schwartz

Printed in the United States of America

10 9 8 7 6 5 4 3 2 1

For

Marie Zazzi

and the memory of

her mother and father

Contents

Acknowledgments   ix

Introduction   xi

Antipasti and Soups   1

Start off your meal the Italian way with a light first course or savory soup. Consider serving these wonderful recipes American style, too, as cocktail-time nibbles (Roasted Eggplant Bruschetta would be delicious with a glass of wine) or light supper (just add salad and crusty bread to Rice, Sweet Pepper, and Shrimp Soup). meat, veggies, and even fruit make soups great for lunch

Pasta, Polenta, Gnocchi, and Risotto   35

While Italian cooks often serve the pasta dish before the main course, Americans love it as the star of the meal. Have fun choosing between Spaghetti with Rosemary Tomato Cream, Baked Penne with Fontina and Mushrooms, and Marie's Gorgonzola Pasta with Pine Nuts.

Seafood   71

In these simple recipes, a handful of ingredients is combined with fish and shellfish to allow the bright, clean seafood flavor to shine through. From elegant Oven-Roasted Scallops with Capers and White Wine to rustic Steamed Clams with Garlic and Olive Oil, you'll find special dishes fit for a company as well as for everyday fare.

Chicken and Turkey 95

talians have a special affinity for poultry, that endlessly versatile ingredient. Savor the earthy flavor of Chicken Marsala and Mushrooms, the spiciness of Chicken Diavolo, and the classic, tomato-sauced Chicken Cacciatore.

Beef, Lamb, Pork, and Veal 121

Here's a collection of satisfyingly hearty dishes for the meat lover. Comfort food is well-represented with Old-Fashioned Meatballs in Red Sauce, Sausages with Cannellini Beans and Tomatoes, and Pot Roast with Red Wine, Italian Style. Or make a sizzling supper from Grilled Steak, Tuscan Style.

Salads 151

Enjoy these refreshing salads in the Italian manner as an antipasto or side dish, or as an American lunch. Try Italian-Style Potato Salad, an old favorite with a Meditteranean twist, or the colorful Summer Sweet Pepper, Tomato, and Onion Salad with Basil.

Side Dishes 171

Italians call side dishes *contorni*, which means contours, as they "round out" the main course. In any language, offerings such as Spinach with Mascarpone, Green Beans with Radicchio, and Arborio Rice Pilaf with Porcini Mushrooms are easy and delicious.

Desserts 203

Perhaps the best illustration of the Italian "less is more" approach to cooking are the sensational desserts. Partake in *la dolce vita* with fragrant Peaches in Red Wine with Almonds, or indulge in the intensely flavored Chocolate Marsala Cake.

Index 225

Acknowledgments

There are four people, above all, I want to thank for helping me create this book. With open, generous hearts, they shared their ideas, time, feedback, and recipes. I thank each of them from the bottom of my heart:

Marie Zazzi

Diana Zazzi, or simply Zazzi, as she likes to be called

Rick Rodgers

Lora Brody

And so many thanks to the special others who played an important role in nurturing this book to fruition:

Philip, my love forever

Rachel, my beautiful daughter who makes me laugh when I think I am not able

Bob, my super smart son-in-law and his welcome, discerning appetite

Sue Davis, Kate Johnson, and Ruth Rosenblum for cheering on The Simpler The Better concept from day one

Steve and Susan Eisenberg, all-time buddies

Margaret Roccanova, for her insight and family recipes

Rachel Spector, always a help and always a sweetheart

Natalie Chapman, Monique Calello, Brenda Blot, and the many other people at John Wiley & Sons who worked on the book, though I never met them

Barbara Kafka, for pointing out that my title The Simpler The Better was a keeper when I first blurted out the phrase

Daune Winfield, my photographer

And finally, to wonderful Susan Wyler, who started me off on a solid footing and stayed around to become a friend. And to editor Pam Chirls, for stepping in with such grace when she was needed. And most dearly to Susan Ginsburg, my agent, who shines with kindness, love, and limitless generosity.

Introduction

My passionate love affair with Italian cooking began well before my first trip to that country of simply prepared, incredibly flavorful food.

I grew up during a period when a home cook's repertoire of Italian dishes included spaghetti and meatballs (if one was lucky), and not much else. In most kitchens, bold and lusty fresh garlic was criminally replaced with garlic powder. The only fresh herb was parsley—the spicy fragrance of fresh basil, an aroma that makes my mouth water even as I simply write about it, was unknown to most Americans. A few years later, when I attended culinary school, we were taught the rigid, classic French approach to cuisine, with barely a nod to the other Mediterranean cultures and the treasures they had to offer to both cooks and diners. When I started working in earnest, at one of the world's biggest hotels, the customers wanted fancy food, and that meant French.

Because I was a curious cook, I occasionally broke away from the yoke of my Francophilia. I began making dishes from the books of such respected trailblazers as Marcella Hazan and Guiliano Bugialli. The flavors sang out to me like opera arias. Some recipes, such as homemade ravioli, with from-scratch pasta, filling, and sauce, were as florid as Baroque arioso, and I appreciated the learning process of making them. However, I was more attracted to dishes with the straightforward, uncomplicated line of a Puccini melody—sautéed chicken breast topped with a slice of prosciutto and a bit of cheese melted on top; asparagus dipped in a warm bath of olive oil, anchovies, and garlic; ribbons of pasta tossed with cream, butter, and Parmesan cheese.

My education in Italian cooking took a quantum leap when Marie Zazzi came into my life. I was running the kitchen at P. S. 77, a restaurant on New York's Upper West Side. Marie became my right hand, my sous chef, my soul mate, and as it turned out, my patron saint of Italian cooking.

Marie comes from an Italian family where food was not just something to eat, but rather, something to celebrate. It was also quite literally their way of life, for the Zazzis, originally from Parma, owned a "continental" restaurant in New York, Chez Cardinal on East 52nd Street. (Curiously enough, or to illustrate my point about the stranglehold French cuisine had on upscale cooking at that time, the restaurant did not have an Italian name, as it was considered too lowbrow for that neighborhood.) Although the restaurant closed when Marie was small, the Zazzis and their extended family cooked as easily as they breathed, even without paying customers.

Here I was, a professional chef classically trained in the French style, yet the seemingly effortless cooking of the Zazzis never failed to impress me. Gradually, I noticed their influence on my cooking. An example is the chicken in rosemary sauce that I would make almost every night as the staff meal. It was the kind of unfettered cooking that I never would have attempted without Marie's example. From there, my flirtation with Italian cooking became more serious. Even after Marie and I stopped working together, our conversations were stuffed with recipes, usually seasoned with reminiscences of Zazzi family feasts.

Quite a few years later, my husband, who was a theatrical agent, was invited to Rome to visit a client making a movie there. With visions of Fellini's *La Dolce Vita* dancing in my head, off we flew together to the land of my culinary dreams. So many of the foods I ate there were revelatory. I remember a bag of roasted chestnuts at the Piazza Navona—perfectly crisp shells nestling the creamy hot flesh, mealy and sweet and divine. Even though I am normally not an espresso aficionado, I lingered over the tiny cups of intensely flavored coffee in cafes, savoring the roasted aroma.

I'll never forget the first time I had *cacio e pepe* at a trattoria in the Trastevere. It was nothing more than a bowl of spaghetti with some grated cheese (*cacio*) and lots of coarsely ground pepper (*pepe*)—pretty unassuming, right? The first impression was the texture of the pasta, perfectly firm-tender, the ultimate example of the elusive concept of *al dente*. Then the flavors revealed themselves, with slightly gamy pecorino Romano matched note for note by the sassy pepper, all held together with the best butter I had ever experienced. The balance achieved absolute bliss, and did so with only four ingredients. To someone raised on spaghetti with tomato sauce, this was an entirely new way to look at pasta. Later in the trip, when I would see an equally perfect piece of art without a single extraneous brush stroke or chisel mark, I sometimes thought of that *cacio e pepe*.

Now that I cook exclusively at home, I find myself returning again and again to the down-to-earth cooking of Italy. In this book, where I expand upon my *The Simpler The Better* format of the previous book in this series, I share my favorite easy Italian recipes, as well as adaptations of my friends' best dishes. Each dish includes Variations for the times when you want a change of pace, and Simple Tips to make the cooking go even more quickly with recommendations for shopping or preparation. Where appropriate with main courses, I also offer Serving Suggestions for side dishes.

If this book gives you a fraction of the joy and satisfaction that I have had cooking Italian style, then I will be as satisfied as I was after my first bowl of *cacio e pepe*. Well, *almost* as satisfied.

The Simpler The Better

Sensational Italian Meals

the simpler the better Antipasti and Soups

Asparagus with Orange and Parmesan Shavings   2

Basil and Olive Oil Dip   4

Roasted Eggplant Bruschetta   6

Goat Cheese with Grapes and Balsamic Vinegar   8

Rosemary-Pepper Pizza Bread   10

Shrimp with Lemon and Garlic   12

Zucchini with Lemon   14

Other Antipasti Ideas   16

Chickpea and Escarole Soup   18

Cannellini Bean and Prosciutto Soup   20

Fontina and Bread Soup   22

Green Beans and Greens Soup   24

Puree of Lentil and Spinach Soup   26

Rice, Sweet Pepper, and Shrimp Soup   28

Tomato, Basil, and Bread Soup   30

Tortellini en Brodo   32

Asparagus with Orange and Parmesan Shavings

Roasted asparagus is so good, it's a wonder that anyone steams it any-more. I just toss them in olive oil, pop them into the oven, and squeeze some orange juice over the top before serving. You won't need additional olive oil, as the amount used in roasting is just enough. It's best to serve the asparagus right after adding the orange juice so its acid doesn't get a chance to discolor the spears. Any size asparagus work well, thick or thin—simply adjust the cooking time as needed.

2 pounds asparagus
2 tablespoons extra-virgin olive oil
1 navel orange
A chunk of imported Parmesan cheese, for shaving

1　Preheat oven to 400°F. Snap off and discard woody stems of asparagus. Place spears on large ungreased baking sheet. Drizzle with olive oil and toss well to coat. Spread spears in single layer, leaving a little room between each.

2　Roast until asparagus is tender but retains a slightly crisp bite, 10 to 15 minutes, depending on size. Transfer to serving platter. Cool to room temperature.

3 Using fine perforations of zester, grate zest of $\frac{1}{2}$ orange. Sprinkle over asparagus, tossing lightly to coat. Cut orange in half. Squeeze, then drizzle 3 tablespoons juice over asparagus. Season with salt and pepper to taste. Using vegetable peeler, shave 8 to 10 Parmesan curls on top of asparagus. Serve right away.

4 SERVINGS

other ideas

SIMPLE TIP *If you have a microplane zester, by all means use it here. You can grate the zest directly over the spears and the little orange wisps will fall and cling right onto the asparagus.*

VARIATIONS *Use fresh lemon zest and lemon juice instead of the orange, but use about 1 tablespoon less of the juice as it's harsher.*

Grilled asparagus is delicious, too. Grill the spears over glowing charcoal, laying them across the rack, or use a ridged grill pan on top of the stove.

Instead of Parmesan cheese shavings, sprinkle the top of the orange-dressed asparagus with about 2 ounces of very thinly sliced prosciutto, cut into strips.

Basil and Olive Oil Dip

This version of the classic oil for dipping raw vegetables and bread, *bagna cauda,* is actually a beautiful green hybrid containing olive oil, basil, garlic, and anchovies. Classic *bagna cauda* is served hot, but this vibrant version is good at room temperature. So serve it, then sit back and relax. Served from a small bowl, it's accompanied with a platter of assorted raw vegetables, such as slivers of fennel bulb, carrot sticks, strips of bell peppers, and spinach leaves and small radishes, both with their stems left on for dipping. And of course, bread. Need I say, the crustier the better?

1 large garlic clove
$3/4$ cup packed basil leaves
4 anchovy fillets in oil, drained
$1/2$ cup extra-virgin olive oil
$1/8$ teaspoon crushed red pepper flakes, or to taste
Assorted raw vegetables and crusty bread

1   With machine running, drop garlic through feed tube of food processor or hole of blender lid. Add basil and anchovies and process until basil is finely chopped.

2   With machine running, gradually add olive oil. Add red pepper flakes and pulse to combine. Carefully season with salt—the anchovies will probably have provided enough.

3   Pour and scrape with rubber spatula from processor into a small bowl. Serve with vegetables and bread for dipping.

MAKES ABOUT ³/₄ CUP, 6 SERVINGS

other ideas

SIMPLE TIPS *If not serving the dip right away, cover it tightly with plastic wrap. The dip will darken as it is exposed to the air, so it looks best and tastes best served the day it's made. Just be sure to stir it well before serving.*

Most supermarkets sell an assortment of raw vegetables cut for crudités. So bring them home, make the dip, and all that's left is to arrange the vegetables on a pretty platter.

DRESS IT UP *Omit the anchovies. And just before serving, drizzle the top of the dip with a few drops of white truffle oil. It's magical, powerful stuff so don't use too much— about ¹/₂ teaspoon will go a long way. I confess I have rarely seen truffle oil in a super- market, but Italian delis and specialty stores often carry it.*

VARIATION *Yes, you can leave out the anchovies if you like. But you might also begin to think of these little fish as an authentic Italian seasoning that is used to deepen the flavor of the dish they're in and cleverly salt it. The trick is to add them in just the right amount, so they season the food without overpowering it. Their presence should be so generally unas- suming, your guests may say "what's that mysterious, delicious taste?"*

Roasted Eggplant Bruschetta

A roasted eggplant collapses in the oven and its insides get squishy. And when you cut it open, the seedy beige flesh doesn't look terribly promising. But then when you chop it and give it a quick sauté with garlic that had been roasted alongside and stir in dribbles of olive oil, it turns creamy and light. Chopped fresh basil is the finishing touch and it becomes a lovely spread for bruschetta—pieces of toast or bread lightly grilled over charcoal.

1$^1/_2$-pound eggplant

5 large garlic cloves, unpeeled

3 tablespoons extra-virgin olive oil

2 tablespoons chopped fresh basil

12 to 18 slices country-style bread, each about 2 x 2 inches

1 Preheat oven to 425°F. Pierce eggplant in 3 or 4 places with sharp fork. Place in baking pan with garlic cloves. Roast, turning garlic occasionally, removing cloves when they feel soft when squeezed, 35 to 40 minutes. Let garlic cool to warm. Trim one end of each clove and squeeze out flesh. Finely chop garlic.

2 Remove eggplant when it starts to collapse, about 10 minutes longer. Let cool enough to handle. Cut in half lengthwise. Discard top long seed strands. Scrape out, then chop remaining flesh; there should be about 1 cup. Discard skin.

3 Heat 1 tablespoon olive oil in large skillet over medium heat. Stir in eggplant and garlic. Reduce heat to low and cook, stirring occasionally, until liquid evaporates, about 5 minutes. Gradually stir in remaining 2 tablespoons oil until eggplant lightens in color and turns creamy, 1 to 2 minutes. Season with salt and pepper to taste. Cool, then stir in basil. Toast bread or grill over charcoal and spread with eggplant. Set bruschetta on a platter and serve.

4 TO 6 SERVINGS

other ideas

DRESS IT UP *Make a mound of the eggplant on a red-tipped lettuce leaf or two on a pretty platter and circle with green and black Mediterranean olives and thin wedges of fresh tomato. Serve with a napkin-lined basket holding toasted slices of country-style bread, ciabatta, and thinly sliced foccacia, if you like.*

VARIATION *Serve the eggplant on a plate surrounded by the toast so each person can make his own. Or serve slices of untoasted country-style bread.*

Goat Cheese with Grapes and Balsamic Vinegar

The grapes are first cut in half to expose their juicy middles, then they get tossed with a little vinegar and olive oil. The combination makes a sweet and tangy antipasto when spooned over goat cheese.

4 ounces goat cheese, preferably caprini
1 cup red or green seedless grapes (6 ounces)
2 teaspoons extra-virgin olive oil
1$^1/_2$ teaspoons balsamic vinegar
Sliced Italian bread for serving

1   Place cheese on serving platter. Cut grapes in half lengthwise.

2   Toss grapes in small bowl with olive oil and vinegar. Season lightly with salt.

3   Spoon grapes over and around cheese. Grind pepper over top and serve with slices of Italian bread.

4 SERVINGS

SIMPLE TIPS *Caprini is a delicious Italian log-style goat cheese that occasionally makes its way into our markets. If you see it, buy two for the recipe. The narrow logs come wrapped in paper and each weighs 2 ounces.*

Cheese is its most flavorful when served at room temperature. Let the goat cheese sit, covered, for at least an hour before preparing the grapes and serving.

Rosemary-Pepper Pizza Bread

Use fresh pizza dough from the refrigerated dairy case to make these. And don't be concerned if your finished breads don't look all that round. Part of the charm is in their irregular shape.

Flour
1 pound pizza dough
2 tablespoons olive oil
1 1/2 teaspoons dried rosemary

1   Preheat oven to 425°F. Flour the rolling surface. Doing half at a time, roll or stretch the dough into an 8-inch circle. Transfer to a lightly floured cookie sheet.

2   Brush top with 1 tablespoon olive oil, then sprinkle with 3/4 teaspoon rosemary. Season with a big pinch of salt and 6 grinds of pepper. Roll out and repeat with other half.

3   Bake breads, puncturing with a sharp knife if they balloon, until tops are light gold, 12 to 15 minutes. Serve warm or at room temperature, cut into wedges.

MAKES TWO 8-INCH BREADS

SIMPLE TIPS *An easy way to roll out the dough is not to roll it at all. Start by pushing the dough into a small, rough circle. Then pick it up by an edge and let it hang from your fingers. Gravity will pull it down, and as you keep turning the dough it will form something of a circle.*

You may also find frozen pizza dough at the supermarket. Thaw according to package directions (usually overnight in the refrigerator) before using.

VARIATION *The possibilities are practically endless, of course: grated Parmesan or a little shredded Fontina or provolone cheese. Slivers of sun-dried tomato or the thinnest slices of fresh tomato. Just think pizza and you'll come up with a dozen more.*

Shrimp with Lemon and Garlic

Shrimp cooked in garlic and olive oil is traditionally Roman. Usually, though, the shrimp are first cooked in an aromatic liquid while still in their shells. Then they're tossed with oil and garlic and when served, everyone peels his own. In this version, already cleaned shrimp are simmered together with garlic-infused olive oil and a handful of thinly sliced celery for contrast. Then a shot of lemon juice is added to the pan juices that adds a nice note of sharpness and makes the shrimp all ready to eat. With some good bread alongside for sopping, of course.

1 pound medium shrimp, peeled and deveined
1 celery stalk
$\frac{1}{3}$ cup extra-virgin olive oil
6 lightly crushed large garlic cloves
2 tablespoons freshly squeezed lemon juice

1 Dry shrimp on paper towels. Thinly slice celery.

2 Set large skillet over low heat with olive oil, garlic, and celery. Cook, stirring occasionally, until garlic is golden all over, 8 to 10 minutes. Discard garlic.

3 Stir in shrimp, cover, and cook over low heat until just cooked through, about 3 minutes. Remove from heat and stir in lemon juice. Season to taste with salt and pepper. Serve at room temperature.

4 SERVINGS

other ideas

SIMPLE TIP *If the shrimp are large, cut them across into halves or thirds before cooking.*

DRESS IT UP *Lay whole, pretty lettuce leaves like Boston or Bibb in a shallow pottery or porcelain dish with the shrimp and juices on top.*

Spoon each serving of shrimp (or shrimp and scallops) over a slice of toasted Italian bread. Spoon their juices over the top, sprinkle with parsley, and serve as a first course or light lunch.

VARIATIONS *Add a pinch of crushed red pepper flakes for heat.*

Use half shrimp and half bay scallops (or sea scallops cut into quarters), adding them the last minute or two.

Toss the shrimp or shrimp and scallops with coarsely chopped parsley when serving.

Zucchini with Lemon

Adapted from friend Margaret Roccanova's family recipe, these zucchini are served as a "first plate" in their Southern Italian–American home. In fact, all their vegetables are served first. The meat, poultry, or fish main course is the second plate and the meal ends with a salad. These lightly puckery zucchini offer a small bite to start, and they enhance one's appetite for the "serious" stuff to come. Particularly if you include bread for sopping up their delicious, lemony, olive oily juices.

1 pound zucchini (3 medium)

2 garlic cloves

2 tablespoons extra-virgin olive oil

1 tablespoon freshly squeezed lemon juice

1 1/2 tablespoons chopped parsley

1 Scrub zucchini well with vegetable brush. Dry on paper towels. Trim and discard ends. Cut each in half lengthwise. Cut each half into 1-inch-thick diagonal pieces. Thinly slice garlic lengthwise.

2 Heat large skillet over medium heat with olive oil. Add zucchini to fit in 1 layer and brown lightly, stirring occasionally, 3 minutes. Stir in garlic and cook until just begins

to turn gold, 30 to 60 seconds. Add $^1/_4$ cup water, cover, and cook until zucchini is tender and water evaporated, 4 or 5 minutes. Remove skillet from heat.

3 Stir in lemon juice and season generously with salt and pepper. Serve warm or at room temperature, stirring in parsley just before serving.

4 SERVINGS

other ideas

SIMPLE TIPS *To purchase the freshest zucchini, squeeze it all along its length. It should be very firm and dense with no soft spots or discoloration. Small to medium-size zucchini have the sweetest taste and the smallest seeds.*

If the water has boiled off before the zucchini are tender, add a few more tablespoons and continue to cook. Or, if there is water left when the zucchini are tender, remove the zucchini from the pan and cook it away, then return the zucchini and stir in the lemon juice.

Cool the zucchini in a shallow bowl or dish so it doesn't continue to cook in its own steam. It will absorb more of its flavorful juices, too.

DRESS IT UP *Present the zucchini with a dollop of fresh, creamy ricotta cheese on top and sprinkle with finely shredded basil.*

VARIATION *Drape strips of roasted red bell peppers over the zucchini when serving. It adds color and extends the amount. For more ideas for expanding this simple plate into something substantial, see page 16.*

Other Antipasti Ideas

All of the vegetable dishes that follow are taken from the book's vegetable and salad chapters, and each is just as good when served as an antipasto or as part of a selection. Warm or at room temperature (or lightly chilled, for seafood) are the best temperatures for serving because the flavors will be most vivid.

FROM THE SIMPLER THE BETTER

Artichoke Hearts with Onion, Balsamic Vinegar, and Parmesan Cheese, page 172, see Variation

Sautéed Asparagus with Onion and Mint, page 174

Broccoli with Black Olives and Red Wine, page 176

Carrots with Olive Oil and Oregano, page 178

Tossed Cauliflower Salad, page 158

Eggplant with Red Onion and Tomato, page 180, see Variation

Sautéed Mushrooms with Garlic, Olive Oil, and Parsley, page 188

Seafood Salad with Mint and Scallion, page 168

Grilled Summer Squash with Parsley and Oregano, page 194

Shredded Beet and Gorgonzola Salad, page 156

OTHER SIMPLE SUGGESTIONS

Most of these ideas take little work, a few a little work, and some none at all since they come already prepared. Just arrange your selection in a pretty way on an attractive plate.

Raw peas in the pod

Raw shredded carrots dressed in olive oil and lemon juice

Slices or wedges of tomato with basil leaf, or grape or cherry tomatoes wrapped in leaf, drizzled with olive oil

Olives of all kinds

Small marinated mozzarella balls or small wedges of imported Parmesan cheese

Roasted or grilled pepper salad

Prepared marinated artichoke hearts

- *Or a mixture of roasted peppers and artichoke hearts*

Sliced prosciutto, bresaola, or salami

- *Rolled wih piece of roasted pepper, olive, and slivers of Parmesan cut with a vegetable peeler*

Prosciutto with fresh figs or melon

Chunks of canned Italian tuna packed in olive oil, as is, or

- *Mixed with chickpeas or cannellini beans and vinegar*
- *Mixed with red onion*

Chickpeas or cannellini beans dressed in olive oil and vinegar

- *With capers*
- *With fresh oregano or basil*

Frozen or fresh Italian green beans, cooked, then tossed with olive oil, vinegar, garlic, and oregano

Bruschetta (grilled or toasted Italian bread slices):

- *Rubbed with garlic and topped with chopped tomato, basil, and garlic salad*
- *Spread with white beans roughly mashed with olive oil and rosemary*
- *With a slice of mozzarella over bruschetta (which has been rubbed with garlic and drizzled with olive oil) and broiled to melt. With anchovy piece, if you like*
- *Spread with sautéed chicken livers mashed with capers and pepper*

Cooked fish broken into large flakes with dollop of lemon mayonnaise

Hard-boiled egg halves with anchovy fillet over each

Mushrooms stuffed and baked with olives, chopped stems, and grated Romano

Spinach frittata

Boiled potato slices seasoned with salt and pepper (top each slice with a sardine and serve with lemon wedges)

Bread salad with olive oil, vinegar, basil, and tomatoes

Chickpea and Escarole Soup

This rustic soup is just what the doctor ordered for nippy nights. It is full of the nubby texture of chickpeas and satisfying, slightly bitter taste of escarole greens. I like it best served with plenty of freshly grated Parmesan cheese sprinkled over the top. And a basket of thick slices of toast for dipping in olive oil or awaiting a slather of soft, sweet butter.

$1/2$ pound escarole
2 tablespoons extra-virgin olive oil
1 large garlic clove, chopped
One 19-ounce can chickpeas
One $14 1/2$-ounce can chicken broth ($1^3/_4$ cups)

1 Discard any discolored outer escarole leaves. Trim stems, then cut escarole lengthwise into quarters. Cut across each into $1/2$-inch-wide strips. Wash and drain well. Heat olive oil over medium heat in large saucepan. Cook garlic, stirring, 15 seconds.

2 Add escarole and cook, stirring occasionally, until wilted, liquid is evaporated, and leaves begin to fry, 8 to 10 minutes. Season with salt to taste.

3 Add chickpeas and juices. Add broth. Bring to boil over high heat and immediately reduce to low. Simmer until escarole is tender, 8 to 10 minutes. Season with pepper and serve hot.

4 SERVINGS

other ideas

VARIATIONS *For a creamier and more elegant version, substitute a can of cannellini beans for the chickpeas.*

Use about 4 of the large outer leaves of Romaine lettuce instead of escarole. It's a good use of the less desirable part of that lettuce.

Cannellini Bean and Prosciutto Soup

White beans play a big role in Tuscan cooking, often as part of a luscious soup. This is one of those recipes that seems creamy, but doesn't contain a drop of cream—it's the tenderness of the beans that does the trick. And prosciutto works its magic, too, by infusing the beans with its special meaty flavor. Simmering the garlic without sautéing it first shows a different side of this Italian kitchen workhorse. Finish each serving with a drizzle of extra-virgin olive oil, and you will have a satisfyingly hearty meal in a bowl.

1 medium onion
2 large garlic cloves
One 3-ounce slice (about $1/8$ inch thick) prosciutto
Two $15\,1/4$- or 19-ounce cans cannellini beans
1 tablespoon extra-virgin olive oil, plus more for serving
one $14\,1/2$-ounce can chicken broth ($1\,3/4$ cups)
$3/4$ teaspoon dried rubbed sage

1   Chop onion. Lightly crush garlic cloves with side of large knife and discard skin. Chop prosciutto into about $1/4$-inch dice. Drain and rinse cannellini beans. Heat 1 table-

spoon olive oil in large saucepan over medium heat. Add onion and prosciutto and cook, stirring often, until onion begins to brown around edges, 10 to 12 minutes.

2   Stir in beans, broth, 1 cup water, sage, and garlic. Bring to boil over high heat. Reduce heat to low and partially cover pot. Simmer until garlic is very tender, about 30 minutes.

3   Mash beans with a potato masher or large slotted spoon to make a thick, chunky soup. Season with salt and pepper to taste. Serve hot, topping each serving with a drizzle of olive oil.

6 SERVINGS

other ideas

SIMPLE TIP *The difference in the amount of beans in a 15$^1\!/_4$-ounce and a 19-ounce can is actually negligible. The extra weight is made up mostly of liquid. How about that!*

VARIATIONS *Use 2 teaspoons chopped fresh sage instead of dried. Or substitute fresh or dried oregano for the sage.*

Set a toasted slice of crusty bread in each bowl before ladling in the soup.

Pass freshly grated Parmesan cheese at the table for spooning onto the soup.

Fontina and Bread Soup

Good cheese, good broth, and bread with character together make a wonderful Italian soup that will definitely remind you of French onion soup—but one that doesn't get, or need, any onions. These irresistible bowlfuls are constructed of 2 layers of buttered toast covered with shredded Fontina cheese. Then boiling hot broth is poured over just before serving to turn the cheese into molten rivulets that run into the broth and fill it with chew and flavor.

2 tablespoons butter
$1/2$ pound lean ground beef, crumbled
5 cups chicken broth
Eight $1/2$-inch-thick slices Italian or country-style bread, each about 3 x 3 inches
2 cups shredded Fontina d'Aosta cheese (about 7 ounces)

1   Melt 1 tablespoon butter in large saucepan over medium heat. Add beef and brown, stirring occasionally, 1 to 2 minutes. Add broth. Reduce heat to medium-low and simmer until flavorful, 8 to 10 minutes, skimming off froth that rises to surface.

2   Strain broth and discard meat. Return broth to saucepan and season with salt to taste.

3 Toast bread. Butter one side of each with remaining 1 tablespoon butter. Lay a slice in each bowl. Cover with $1/4$ cup cheese. Top or overlap with second slice and cover each with remaining cheese. Bring broth to quick boil over high heat and pour over toasts. Grind pepper over top and serve immediately.

4 SERVINGS

other ideas

SIMPLE TIP *Real Fontina d'Aosta can be hard to find, though better supermarkets do carry it. You may also find a Fontina from Italy that isn't from the Val d'Aosta region. It has a more processed texture and taste but is more flavorful than the Fontina that comes from Sweden. Or substitute Swiss or French Gruyère. Or Muenster with a handful of grated Parmesan.*

Green Beans and Greens Soup

This simple rustic soup is made up of green beans, chard, and potato that all turn tender and soft once the soup is ready to eat. Underlying their earthy vegetableness is meaty flavor thanks to a few simmering chunks of prosciutto, there for the greater good of the soup. When served, I like to see that the once-bright greens have dulled in color because it says their flavor has fully developed inside the pot. Grated Parmesan served on the side for sprinkling is a good addition, or try shredded sharp provolone or mozzarella strewn over their tops.

3-ounce chunk prosciutto, preferably cut from shank end

1 medium onion

3 garlic cloves

$1/2$ pound green beans

1 pound chard or beet greens, coarse stems trimmed

1 medium to large boiling potato

2 tablespoons butter

One 14$1/2$-ounce can chicken broth (1$3/4$ cups)

1   Cut prosciutto into 4 pieces. Chop onion and garlic. Snap ends, then cut green beans

into 1-inch lengths. Wash greens, dry, and chop. Peel potato, cut into ¹/₂-inch dice, and keep in bowl covered by cold water.

2 Melt butter in large saucepan over medium heat. Add prosciutto, onion, and garlic. Cook, stirring occasionally, until onion and garlic begin to turn translucent but do not brown, about 3 minutes. Stir in green beans and greens. Stew together, uncovered, stirring occasionally, about 10 minutes. Drain potato and add to pot. Add broth plus ¹/₂ cup hot water. Simmer until potato is tender, about 15 minutes.

3 Discard prosciutto pieces. Season generously with salt and pepper. Serve hot.

4 SERVINGS

other ideas

SIMPLE TIP *Dry the greens well so the soup flavor doesn't become diluted.*

DRESS IT UP *When serving, dress up the soup with fresh basil in one of three ways: (1) Add chopped leaves to each bowlful. (2) Puree a handful of leaves with a little olive oil in a blender, then drizzle the green oil over the tops. (3) Spoon a dollop of pesto over each serving.*

VARIATIONS *Replace the butter and prosciutto with bacon fat alone or the prosciutto with a few chunks of smoked ham.*

Leave out the meat and make the soup with vegetable broth.

Add a rind of Parmesan or two to the soup as it cooks instead of serving grated cheese on the side.

Puree of Lentil and Spinach Soup

This soup embodies one of my favorite qualities of Italian food: its effortless ability to be both elegant and rustic at the same time. In this case, lentils and spinach, with a few hunks of prosciutto, all simmer together to create a deeply flavorful, down-to-earth soup. And then the blender gets to work and they become a puree as smooth as velvet. Yet somehow the blending changes more than the form of the soup. It adds refinement, without losing an iota of its earthiness.

3-ounce prosciutto chunk, preferably cut from shank end

3 tablespoons extra-virgin olive oil

1 medium onion, chopped

2 large garlic cloves, minced

One 9-ounce bag washed spinach

$^2/_3$ cup lentils

1 Cut prosciutto into 2 or 3 pieces. Heat olive oil in soup pot over medium-low. Add prosciutto and brown, turning occasionally, about 3 minutes. Stir in onion and garlic and cook until light gold, 5 to 6 minutes. Stir in spinach and cook until thoroughly wilted, 1 to 2 minutes.

2   Rinse lentils, drain, and add to pot. Add 1 quart water and bring to boil over medium-high heat. Immediately reduce heat to low. Simmer soup, partially covered, until lentils are tender, about 30 minutes.

3   Discard prosciutto pieces. Doing in batches, puree soup in blender until very smooth. Season with salt to taste. Ladle into bowls and grind fresh pepper over each serving.

4 TO 6 SERVINGS

other ideas

SIMPLE TIP *The shank portion of a prosciutto is too tough for slicing, but it has lots of flavor. Savory cooks buy a nice hunk of the meaty shank to use for flavoring soups. Cut it into small chunks and freeze them for whenever you want a piece or two. When ready to use, defrost them in the microwave first or simply cook them a bit longer in olive oil before adding the other ingredients.*

DRESS IT UP *In addition to the fresh pepper, scatter a few slivers of prosciutto, freshly cut from the prime slicing part, over each bowlful. And float a leaf of fresh parsley or basil over top, too.*

VARIATIONS *For a more rustic soup, coarsely chop the spinach before adding it to the pot. Then puree only a ladle or two of the soup when it's done so you will have a pleasing contrast of textures.*

Sprinkle each serving with freshly grated imported Parmesan cheese instead of a grinding of pepper.

Rice, Sweet Pepper, and Shrimp Soup

Lots of tender white rice and pieces of pink shrimp and red pepper make this delicate soup pretty to look at and easy to eat. And while the soup is a brothy one, it also has a lightly creamy quality from the Italian rice. The rice is cooked first in just the amount of broth it can absorb to help bring out its natural starchiness. Then more broth is stirred in along with the shrimp to simmer and finish.

12 medium shrimp, peeled and deveined (about 6 ounces)

$^1/_2$ small onion

$^1/_2$ medium red bell pepper

2 tablespoons butter

$^2/_3$ cup Italian arborio rice

3 cups chicken broth

$^1/_2$ teaspoon finely chopped fresh rosemary

1 Cut shrimp across into $^1/_2$-inch pieces. Chop onion and bell pepper into somewhat smaller pieces. Melt butter in large saucepan over low heat. Stir in onion, bell pepper, and rice. Cook, stirring occasionally, until onion begins to turn translucent, about 5 minutes.

2   Increase heat to medium and gradually stir in 1³/₄ cups broth. Bring to simmer, stirring occasionally. Cover and cook until liquid is absorbed and rice tender, 12 to 14 minutes.

3   Stir in remaining 1¹/₄ cups broth and rosemary. Return to simmer, stir in shrimp, and cook until they turn opaque, 1 to 2 minutes. Season with salt and pepper to taste and serve hot.

4 SERVINGS

other ideas

DRESS IT UP *Replace the shrimp with jumbo lump crab meat or pieces of cooked lobster meat added the last minute to heat through.*

Stir in a little cream to finish and sprinkle each serving with torn fresh basil leaves or chopped fennel greens.

VARIATIONS *Use another short or medium-grain rice instead of arborio.*

Replace the rosemary with a good pinch of dried marjoram.

Add a chopped garlic clove to the vegetables in their last minute of cooking.

Replace the shrimp with small pieces of raw fish fillet, chopped shucked clams, or scallops.

Tomato, Basil, and Bread Soup

This soup is a Tuscan classic, but the word *soup* doesn't really begin to describe *pappa di pomodoro*! Basically, it is a fresh basil-scented tomato soup thickened with day-old bread whose sturdy texture may seem unusual if you haven't tasted it before. But just you wait until the bread starts soaking up the soup and all the good flavors of tomato, olive oil, and basil come together on your taste buds.

1 medium onion

2 garlic cloves

$2^{1}/_{2}$ tablespoons extra-virgin olive oil

One 28-ounce can diced tomatoes in juice

3 cups chicken broth

$^{1}/_{4}$ cup chopped fresh basil

1 to $1^{1}/_{2}$ cups day-old Italian bread, broken into bite-size pieces

1 Chop onion. Mince garlic. Heat 1 tablespoon olive oil in large saucepan over medium heat. Add onion and cook, stirring often, until golden, about 5 minutes. Add garlic and cook until fragrant and just turning light gold, about 1 minute.

2 Stir in tomatoes with their juices, the broth, and 1 cup water. Bring to a boil over high

heat, stirring once or twice. Reduce heat to low and partially cover pot. Simmer for 30 minutes, stirring occasionally, until lightly thickened.

3 Stir in 2 tablespoons basil. Cook, uncovered, stirring occasionally, about 1 minute. Scatter bread pieces over the soup. Ladle into bowls, garnish each with its share of the remaining 2 tablespoons basil, and drizzle with remaining $1^1/_2$ tablespoons olive oil. Serve hot.

4 SERVINGS

other ideas

SIMPLE TIP *For the bread, use any firm, crusty bread, including whole grain. But don't use sourdough—its tanginess fights the taste of the tomatoes.*

VARIATIONS *Instead of the chopped basil, stir a couple of tablespoons prepared store-bought pesto into the soup just before serving. Or, serve each bowlful with a dollop on top.*

Easily turned into a meatless soup, you can simply replace vegetable broth for the chicken broth and the water.

A little spicy heat is easily added with a pinch of crushed red pepper flakes.

Tortellini en Brodo

Homemade meat broth is the foundation for the classic Italian soup, tortellini in broth. But even without taking the time to prepare the "real McCoy," you can make a surprisingly savory alternative with a couple of cans of chicken broth and a little finagling. The trick is to simmer the broth with ground beef just long enough for the beef flavor to combine with the chicken and take away the memory of the can. Then the meat is strained out and the little stuffed pastas are simmered right in the same pot. If you want to do a bit more, and I admit I can't resist the addition, finely chop and sauté a little carrot and onion and add them, too. For how, see Dress It Up.

1 tablespoon butter
$1/2$ pound lean ground beef, crumbled
Two $14 1/2$-ounce cans chicken broth ($3 1/2$ cups)
1 cup fresh green tortellini (about 5 ounces)

1   Melt butter in large saucepan over medium to high heat. Add meat and brown, stirring occasionally, about 1 minute. Stir in broth plus $1/2$ cup water. Reduce heat to medium-low and simmer until flavorful, 8 to 10 minutes, skimming off froth that rises to surface.

2   Strain broth and discard meat. Return broth to saucepan.

3   Add tortellini and simmer over medium-low heat until slightly more cooked than al dente, 3 to 5 minutes. Season with pepper (the broth should provide enough salt). Ladle into bowls and serve hot.

4 SERVINGS

other ideas

SIMPLE TIP *Using ground beef that contains about 8 percent fat (often labeled ground sirloin) will add the beefy flavor without making extra degreasing necessary.*

DRESS IT UP *This soup is particularly good and looks pretty when fresh vegetables are added. Finely chop a medium carrot and a small onion, then cook them in the saucepan in their own tablespoon of butter until lightly brown and tender-crunchy. Set them aside and prepare the soup as above, then add them back to the pot when the tortellini is done.*

the simpler the better # Pasta, Gnocchi, Polenta, and Risotto

Castellane with Eggplant	36
Fresh Fettuccine with Sweet Red Onions and Walnuts	38
Fettuccine with Peas and Pancetta	40
Gemelli with Black Olives, Capers, and Sautéed Bread Crumbs	42
Marie's Gorgonzola Pasta with Pine Nuts	44
Fresh Linguine with Butter, Parmesan Cheese, and Mushrooms	46
Orechiette with Sausage and Sweet Red Peppers	48
Mini-Rigatoni with Red Wine Ragù	50
Spaghetti with Rosemary Tomato Cream	52
Peppery Spaghetti with Romano Cheese	54
Spaghetti with Grape Tomatoes and Pesto	56
Potato Gnocchi with Black Olive Pesto	58
Potato Gnocchi with Butter, Tomato, and Sage	60
Polenta with Cheese and Walnuts	62
Polenta with Zia Pia's Salami Sauce	64
Golden Garlic and Cabbage Risotto	66
Quick Risotto with Tuna and Tomatoes	68

Castellane with Eggplant

This meaty pasta is perfumed with garlic-infused olive oil and loaded with chunks of eggplant. It's also shot through with just enough anchovy to bring in a hint of the sea. And if the shape of castellane isn't familiar to you, imagine a tightly curled, elongated snail and you'll get the picture. I like this pasta best without adding any grated cheese.

2 pounds eggplant

4 large garlic cloves

4 anchovy fillets

$2/3$ cup lightly packed flat-leaf parsley

$3/4$ cup olive oil

1 pound dried castellane, lumache, ziti, or other short pasta

1   Bring a large pot of salted water to a boil. Trim off and discard ends of eggplant. Cut eggplant into $3/4$-inch dice. Lightly crush garlic with the side of a knife. Finely chop anchovies. Lay parsley leaves on top of anchovies and chop together well.

2   Heat $1/2$ cup of the olive oil in a very large skillet over low heat. Add garlic and cook until both sides are golden. Discard garlic. Pour half of garlic oil into a bowl. Increase heat to medium-high. Add half the eggplant. Sauté until browned and just tender,

stirring frequently, 8 to 10 minutes. Remove. Repeat with second half of eggplant in remaining garlic oil.

3 Cook pasta al dente, 13 to 14 minutes. Drain. Add remaining $1/4$ cup unflavored oil to pot over low heat. Stir in anchovy-parsley mixture and cook, stirring, 1 minute. Return pasta to pot with eggplant. Heat 1 minute, stirring. Season with salt and pepper to taste. Serve hot.

4 TO 6 SERVINGS

other ideas

SIMPLE TIP *Here's an efficient and safe way to dice eggplant. First, trim off its ends. Then cut a thin lengthwise slice off any side. Now lay the eggplant on its flat side. Cut the eggplant lengthwise into slices as thick as you want. Stack a few of them at a time on a flat side. Cut them lengthwise into strips. Then cut across the stack to make the size dice you want.*

Fresh Fettuccine with Sweet Red Onions and Walnuts

Red onions need only a few minutes of cooking to draw out their sweet nature. And that's what happens to them here. They're sautéed in a hot pan with olive oil and chopped walnuts, which toast at the same time. For me, the delicate flavor of the finished pasta is best appreciated without adding grated cheese. But I'll leave it up to you.

2 large red onions
$1/2$ cup walnut pieces
$1/3$ cup olive oil
1 pound fresh fettuccine
$2/3$ cup heavy cream

1   Bring a large pot of salted water to a boil for the pasta. Thinly slice onions. Finely chop walnuts.

2   Heat olive oil in a large skillet over medium-high heat. Add onions and nuts. Cook, stirring occasionally, until onions brown lightly but remain somewhat crunchy, about 3 minutes. Remove skillet from heat.

3 Boil pasta until al dente, about 3 minutes. Drain. Add onion-nut mixture and cream to pot over medium-high heat. Let cream thicken lightly, stirring, 1 minute. Reduce heat to low and return pasta to pot. Combine and season with salt and pepper to taste. Serve hot.

4 SERVINGS

other ideas

SIMPLE TIP *The pasta shouldn't stick together in the brief time it sits in the colander. But if you're concerned, toss it with a little olive oil.*

VARIATION *Omit the cream at the end and add enough olive oil to coat the pasta well. Vegetable-flavored pasta such as spinach or beet would be good, too, in place of the plain.*

Fettuccine with Peas and Pancetta

For me, pancetta is one of the most appealing foods created from that invaluable animal, the pig. It's cut from the belly just like bacon, but unlike bacon, pancetta isn't smoked. Instead it's cured with salt and pepper to create its distinctive but delicate taste. Rolled into a big salami shape, it gets thinly sliced when you buy it. In this dish, small pieces are lightly crisped, then tossed with fettuccine, olive oil, and peas. The rich, lightly peppery pork and sweet-tasting peas become entangled with the tender-chewy strands of pasta, then a handful of basil leaves and sprinkle of Parmesan cheese completes this charming jumble of tastes.

4 ounces thinly sliced pancetta

4 garlic cloves

$2/3$ cup extra-virgin olive oil

1 pound dried fettuccine or tagliatelle

One 10-ounce package frozen peas (2 cups)

$3/4$ lightly packed cup fresh basil

1 Unroll pancetta slices, then cut each strip across into pieces about $1/2$ inch wide. Thinly slice garlic.

2 Heat olive oil in a medium skillet over medium-low heat. Add pancetta. Cook, stirring occasionally and pressing down to submerge, until pale gold in color, about 10 minutes. Drain on paper towels. Add garlic to olive oil in skillet and cook over low heat until just turning pale gold, about 1 minute. Remove from heat.

3 Bring a large pot of salted water to a boil over high heat. Cook pasta until almost al dente, about 6 minutes, then add peas to pot. Cook 1 minute more, then drain. Return pot to low heat and add garlic-olive oil. Stir in pasta with peas. Stir in pancetta and toss strands to combine as best as possible. Season with salt and pepper to taste. Transfer to serving dish or divide among plates and scatter basil over top.

4 TO 6 SERVINGS

other ideas

SIMPLE TIPS *The pancetta cuts more easily when the blade of the knife is heated first.*

Pancetta is generally cooked only long enough to turn golden. If it's cooked crisp like bacon, it turns hard.

The garlic will continue to cook in the olive oil from the retained heat of the pan, particularly if the pan is a heavy one. So be sure not to let it get too dark before removing it from the heat.

VARIATION *Cooked diced red bell peppers, carrot slivers, or chopped spinach can be used instead of peas.*

Gemelli with Black Olives, Capers, and Sautéed Bread Crumbs

Gemelli is a tightly curled pasta spiral, perfect for capturing the pungent and briny pieces of olives and capers in this dish. The olive oil–sautéed bread crumbs, referred to in Italy as "poor man's cheese," add a satisfying crunch to this mouth-filling combination of tastes when they're showered over the dish at the last.

$^2/_3$ cup extra-virgin olive oil

$^1/_4$ cup plain dry bread crumbs

4 large garlic cloves

24 dry-cured black olives

1 pound dried gemelli or fusilli

3 tablespoons drained capers

1   Bring a large pot of salted water to a boil. Heat 2 tablespoons olive oil in small skillet over medium-low heat. Add bread crumbs and cook, stirring frequently, until crisp and golden, 4 to 5 minutes. Set aside. Finely sliver garlic. Pit and coarsely chop olives.

2   Cook pasta until al dente, about 7 minutes. Drain and reserve pot. Add remaining olive oil to pasta pot over medium-low heat. Add garlic, olives, and capers. Cook,

stirring occasionally, until garlic turns light gold and mixture is aromatic, 1 to 2 minutes.

3 Return pasta to pot and reduce heat to low. Stir together to reheat pasta and combine flavors, 1 minute. Season with salt to taste and a generous amount of pepper. Divide among plates and sprinkle with toasted bread crumbs.

4 TO 6 SERVINGS

other ideas

SIMPLE TIPS *To cut thin garlic slivers, first cut each clove in half horizontally. Then cut the cloves lengthwise into very thin slivers.*

Pit olives easily by pressing on top of one at a time with the side of a large knife. They will open up just enough so you can pull the pit right out.

VARIATION *Stir in 2 tablespoons of coarsely chopped parsley or basil just before serving.*

Marie's Gorgonzola Pasta with Pine Nuts

Italian Gorgonzola is one of the world's great blue cheeses. Unlike some of the other great ones, such as English Stilton, French Roquefort, and Spanish Cabrales, with their sharper, saltier taste and crumbly consistency, Gorgonzola is smooth and creamy in both texture and flavor. Simply served with perfectly ripe fruit alongside, it can bring a meal to an elegant and satisfying end. Or you can use it in cooking, as my friend Marie does in her cheesy-nutty pasta. She also suggests adding a handful of gorgeous, summer yellow cherry tomatoes to the mix, too, when they're around.

6 ounces Italian Gorgonzola cheese

6 tablespoons butter

1 pound dried penne rigate, penne, or shells

$1/3$ cup pine nuts

$1^1/2$ lightly packed cups fresh basil, torn into bite-size pieces

Freshly grated imported Parmesan cheese

1 Bring a large pot of salted water to a boil over high heat. Coarsely chop enough Gorgonzola to measure $2/3$ cup. Cut butter into 6 pieces. Place cheese and butter in small, heat-resistant bowl and season generously with pepper. Set aside.

2 When water boils, add pasta, stir once, cover, and place bowl of cheese and butter on top to soften and melt. Toast pine nuts in a small, dry skillet over very low heat, rolling them in the pan almost constantly until they have golden brown spots, about 3 minutes. Set aside.

3 Cook the pasta until al dente, then drain. Return it to its cooking pot set over low heat. Stir in cheese-butter mixture and heat together, stirring, 1 minute. Stir in pine nuts and season with salt and pepper to taste. Stir in basil. Divide among dinner plates or serve in a large bowl, family style. Sprinkle with grated cheese and pass additional on the side.

4 TO 6 SERVINGS

other ideas

SIMPLE TIPS *Look on the Gorgonzola label for the words "product of Italy" to be sure you're buying the "real McCoy."*

Marie covers her pasta pot with a cookie sheet so the bowl of cheese and butter sits flat.

DRESS IT UP *By simply changing the pasta you can dress up this dish. Long, fresh noodles such as fettuccine, tagliatelle, or even linguine, whether flavored with spinach, beet, carrot, or just plain, will make it more elegant.*

VARIATION *Coarsely chopped, toasted walnuts or hazelnuts are a good and different-tasting substitute for the pine nuts.*

Fresh Linguine with Butter, Parmesan Cheese, and Mushrooms

Pasta with butter and cheese isn't just a dish for children, though it's often thought of that way here. Actually, you could say it was quite sophisticated because of the purity of the ingredients. But for me, I simply love the comfort of tender, fresh noodles tossed in softened butter and freshly grated Parmesan cheese, and how the strands are coated with gentle, nutty flavor. In this version, I've added a whiff of garlic and a small handful of mushrooms so as you eat, you get an occasional bite filled with woodsy taste.

4 tablespoons butter

$1/4$ pound cremini or white button mushrooms

1 large garlic clove, lightly crushed

12 ounces fresh linguine or other fresh pasta

$1/2$ cup grated Parmesan cheese, plus more for garnish

1   Soften 3 tablespoons of butter. Bring a large pot of salted water to a boil for the pasta. Finely sliver mushrooms.

2   Melt remaining 1 tablespoon butter with garlic in medium saucepan over medium heat. Cook garlic without browning to perfume butter, stirring occasionally, 2 min-

utes. Add mushrooms, season lightly with salt, and cook until tender and giving off liquid, 3 to 4 minutes. Discard garlic.

3 Cook pasta until al dente, 2 to 3 minutes, then drain. Return pasta to hot cooking pot. Toss with mushrooms and liquid and half of grated cheese. Continue tossing with half of softened butter, then remaining cheese. Toss with remaining butter and season with salt to taste. Serve right away with a little fresh pepper on top and grated cheese on the side.

3 SERVINGS

other ideas

SIMPLE TIPS *Soften the butter by cutting it into little pieces, letting it soften slightly, then mashing it in a bowl with the back of a spoon. Or briefly heat a mixing bowl, add the pieces of butter, and mash it.*

Serve the pasta on warmed plates to help keep it hot.

DRESS IT UP *Toss the pasta with sautéed tiny shrimp with or without the mushrooms. Or heat lump crab meat with the mushrooms at the last minute. Scatter diced tomato tossed in butter for a few seconds over either pasta.*

Wild mushrooms such as chanterelles, oyster mushrooms, shiitakes, or hen of the woods are wonderful with the pasta. Garnish each serving with Parmesan shavings cut from the wedge with a vegetable peeler instead of serving extra grated cheese on the side.

VARIATIONS *In place of the mushrooms, top each serving with a spoonful of thinly sliced zucchini that has been cooked in butter until very tender.*

Substitute dried pasta for fresh, adding more butter and cheese if needed.

Orechiette with Sausage and Sweet Red Peppers

Orechiette means "little ears" in Italian, and of course, that's just what this pasta looks like. But far from being insubstantial, the little ears actually offer a good deal of chew and plenty of cavities for capturing the crumbled pieces of sausage and chopped peppers. A generous sprinkle of grated Romano cheese over the top gives it a good finish.

1^1/$_4$ pounds sweet Italian sausage meat

1^1/$_2$ large red bell peppers

^{1}/$_4$ cup extra-virgin olive oil

5 large garlic cloves

1 pound dried orechiette or other short pasta

1 Bring a large pot of salted water to a boil. Break sausage into small pieces. Finely chop bell peppers.

2 Heat olive oil in large skillet over low heat. Add garlic and cook, turning frequently, until golden, 8 to 10 minutes. Discard garlic. Increase heat to high. Add peppers and sausage. Cook, stirring occasionally, until all is lightly crisped and browned, about 10 minutes.

3   Cook pasta until al dente, about 12 minutes. Reserve $1/4$ cup cooking water, then drain. Return pasta to pot and stir in sausage and peppers. Add reserved water to sausage cooking pan and stir up brown residue over low heat. Add drippings to pasta and heat together over low heat 1 minute, stirring occasionally. Season with salt to taste. Serve hot and generously grind pepper over each plateful.

4 SERVINGS

other ideas

SIMPLE TIP *No bulk ground Italian sausage in the market? Then buy links, snip off a bit from each end, and peel away the casings.*

VARIATION *Use a mixture of sweet and hot sausage, or all hot even if you want the biggest kick.*

Mini-Rigatoni with Red Wine Ragù

Ragù, or Bolognese as it's also called, is a rich sauce made from ground meat, a bit of prosciutto or pancetta, tomatoes, chopped vegetables, wine, and often milk for tenderizing the meat. It's traditionally simmered for hours. This quicker, weekday version gets its character from a generous splash of red wine and plenty of tomato. Vegetable broth fills in handily for all the veggies. To give the dish an extra level of taste, I like to heat the just-cooked pasta in olive oil and garlic, then stir in a cupful of the ragù for a last-minute melding of flavors. Then the pasta is divvied among plates, covered with a heap of sauce, and sprinkled with freshly grated Parmesan cheese.

$^1/_4$ cup extra-virgin olive oil

$1^1/_4$ pounds ground chuck

4 garlic cloves, minced

$^1/_2$ cup milk

One $14^1/_2$-ounce can vegetable broth ($1^3/_4$ cups)

$^3/_4$ cup red wine

$1^1/_2$ cups crushed tomatoes in heavy puree

1 pound dried mini-rigatoni or spaghetti

1. Heat 1 tablespoon olive oil over high heat in a large saucepan. Add beef, season lightly with salt, and cook away redness, stirring and breaking up meat with the spoon, about 3 minutes. Stir in three-fourths of the garlic and cook, stirring occasionally, 1 minute. Add milk, lower heat to medium, and cook until mostly absorbed, about 3 minutes. Add broth, wine, and tomatoes. It will look very thin at this point.

2. Bring to a strong simmer over high heat, then reduce heat to low. Simmer, stirring occasionally, until thick and rich, 35 to 45 minutes. Season generously with salt and pepper. Set aside.

3. Bring a large pot of salted water to a boil. Cook pasta until al dente, 8 to 10 minutes. Drain. Return pot to low heat and add remaining 3 tablespoons olive oil and remaining garlic. Cook, stirring, 1 minute. Stir in pasta and heat 1 minute more. Stir in 1 cup ragù and heat together 1 minute. Reheat remaining sauce, if necessary. Divide pasta among plates and top each with a ladleful of sauce.

4 TO 6 SERVINGS

other ideas

SIMPLE TIP *Different brands of canned crushed tomatoes make a difference in the finished ragù. Ones that indicate "concentrate" on the label are puree-like and have no visible pieces of tomato. They make a sauce that turns rich and thick quickly. Brands that contain pieces of tomato in thick, heavy puree take a little longer to become rich and thick but they can boast a somewhat more refined flavor.*

VARIATION *Prepare the sauce with 2 parts ground beef and 1 part ground pork. Or use a packaged meat-loaf mixture of beef, veal, and pork.*

Spaghetti with Rosemary Tomato Cream

Years ago a charming Italian gentleman came to one of the restaurants where I was chef to instruct my staff and me in the proper use of the massive pasta machines we had just acquired. While he was there, we fell into a chat and he happened to mention this dish. To my surprise, he gently insisted I try my hand at it right then and there! I did, and not long after introduced it onto the menu. And now I serve it at home because we love its satisfying character. Accompanied by a bowl of freshly grated Parmesan for sprinkling, of course.

$1\frac{1}{2}$ tablespoons extra-virgin olive oil

1 medium to large onion, chopped

1 teaspoon minced fresh rosemary

$2\frac{1}{4}$ cups canned crushed tomatoes in heavy puree

$\frac{1}{2}$ cup heavy cream

1 pound dried spaghetti or linguine

1 Bring a large pot of salted water to a boil for the pasta.

2 Heat olive oil in a large saucepan over low heat. Add onion and cook, stirring occasionally, until almost translucent, about 3 minutes. Add rosemary and cook 30

seconds. Stir in tomatoes and simmer until onion is tender, 6 to 8 minutes. Stir in cream and simmer until sauce is lightly thickened, 2 to 3 minutes.

3 Cook pasta until al dente, 10 to 12 minutes, then drain. Return pasta to pot over low heat. Stir in sauce and season with salt and pepper to taste. Heat together, stirring, for 30 seconds and serve hot.

4 TO 6 SERVINGS

other ideas

VARIATION *Use $1/2$ teaspoon of crumbled dried rosemary in place of the fresh. Stir in $1/2$ cup chopped parsley just before serving.*

Peppery Spaghetti with Romano Cheese

Here it is, the dish that convinced me that my love affair with Italian food was no passing fancy. It's known as *cacio e pepe,* literally "cheese and pepper," even though pasta certainly plays a big part. Use the absolute best example of each component: artisan Italian pasta (extruded through handmade bronze dies to give it a rough texture that soaks up sauces), true pecorino Romano (keeping in mind that most supermarket "Romano" cheeses are Sardinian or even Argentinian), European-style butter (which has a higher butterfat content than American varieties and is often made with fermented cream to give a hint of tanginess), and freshly ground black pepper (adjust your peppermill to its coarsest setting). The dish will be just fine if you make it with mid-level ingredients, but to really make it sing, splurge on the good stuff.

1 pound spaghetti, preferably an Italian artisan brand (which will come in a 1$^1/_{10}$-pound package, but 1 ounce won't make much difference)

4 tablespoons butter, preferably unsalted European style, such as Plugra, at room temperature

³/₄ cup (3 ounces) freshly grated pecorino Romano cheese, plus more for serving

1¹/₂ teaspoons coarsely ground black pepper

1   Bring a large pot of salted water to a boil. Add pasta and cook, stirring often to be sure spaghetti doesn't stick together, until al dente, about 7 minutes. Scoop out and reserve ¹/₂ cup pasta cooking water. Drain pasta and return to pot.

2   Add butter to pot and toss to melt. Add cheese and pepper and toss, adding enough pasta cooking water to moisten pasta. Serve hot, with additional cheese on the side.

4 TO 6 SERVINGS

other ideas

SIMPLE TIP *A sharp grating cheese made from sheep's milk, real pecorino Romano isn't common, but you will be able to find it at well-stocked markets, cheese stores, and Italian delicatessens that really know their cheeses. Pecorino Romano is moister than pecorino Sardo from Sardinia or Tuscan pecorino Toscano, and was certainly the cheese used in the cacio e pepe that turned my head at that trattoria in Rome. Some pecorino Romano cheeses are embossed with a sheep's head symbol, but more often than not the cheese will simply sport a painted black rind. Reliable brands include Fulvi and Locatelli.*

VARIATIONS *You can use extra-virgin olive oil instead of the butter, if you insist. Actually, it's very good, but the creaminess of the butter combined with the milky characteristics of the cheese seems more correct.*

Leftovers of this dish, savored at room temperature, are wonderful. The rest allows the flavors to marry beautifully.

Spaghetti with Grape Tomatoes and Pesto

Pesto lends its incredibly delicious aroma and flavor to many dishes. Here it is in the role that introduced most of us to its talents—with pasta. Buy pesto from the refrigerated section of the supermarket, as the fresh variety is superior to the bottled version.

1 pound spaghetti

2 tablespoons extra-virgin olive oil

2 pints grape tomatoes

$1/4$ cup pesto

Freshly grated imported Parmesan cheese for serving

1 Bring a large pot of salted water to a boil. Cook spaghetti until al dente, about 9 minutes. Drain, reserving about $1/2$ cup of the cooking water. Set pasta aside; do not rinse.

2 Return pot to stove. Add olive oil and heat over medium-high heat. Add tomatoes and cook, stirring occasionally, until tomatoes begin to split, about 3 minutes.

3 Remove pot from the heat. Add pasta and the pesto. Mix, adding enough reserved cooking water to loosen pesto and create a light sauce. Serve hot, with grated cheese on the side.

4 TO 6 SERVINGS

SIMPLE TIP *To store leftover pesto, spread it evenly in its container with a spatula. Pour a thin layer of extra-virgin olive oil on top (which seals the pesto and keeps more air than the lid alone) and refrigerate. When you want to use the pesto, stir in the oil layer. Stored in this manner, the pesto should keep for a couple of weeks.*

DRESS IT UP *Top each serving with crumbled goat cheese.*

VARIATION *Use a few tablespoons of bottled olive paste, such as tapenade or olivada, instead of the pesto or use the black olive pesto from page 58.*

Potato Gnocchi with Black Olive Pesto

Forgoing the nuts and gentle with garlic, this pesto has olives to give it punch. It's more coarsely ground than the usual version and when it all comes together, the mild dumplings are coated in deep, almost mysterious Mediterranean flavors.

4 Greek black olives, such as Kalamata

1 garlic clove

1 packed cup fresh basil

2 tablespoons extra-virgin olive oil

One 1.1-pound package vacuum-packed potato gnocchi from Italy

2 tablespoons grated Parmesan cheese

1 Bring a large pot of salted water to a boil. Pit and coarsely chop olives. Coarsely chop garlic.

2 Place olives, garlic, and basil in food processor. Finely chop while gradually adding olive oil, about 2 minutes. Scrape down sides occasionally. Transfer to large bowl and stir in 1/4 cup boiling water.

3 Add the gnocchi to water and cook until they rise to surface, 1 to 2 minutes. Drain well. Add to pesto in bowl and toss to coat. Sprinkle with cheese and toss. Season with salt and pepper to taste and serve right away.

4 SERVINGS AS A FIRST COURSE

other ideas

SIMPLE TIPS *Black French olives can be substituted for the Greek olives. The most commonly available ones are Niçoise, and they're quite small, so use about 12.*

Warm the bowl a little before tossing the gnocchi so they don't cool off rapidly. And if you like, warm the plates, too.

Potato Gnocchi with Butter, Tomato, and Sage

the simpler the better

Gnocchi are made with either potatoes, *gnocchi di patate,* or semolina wheat, *gnocchi alla romana.* When made with potatoes, as the ones are here, they're little dumplings about 1 inch long and traditionally served as their own course in place of pasta. But they could become supper along with a salad or vegetable, if you choose. This particular version won't disappoint. The dumplings are first boiled— they take only a minute or two—then glossed with a light, buttery tomato sauce full of sage flavor. Gnocchi are often served with a sprinkle of grated Parmesan, but I don't think these need any.

5 fresh sage leaves

3 tablespoons butter

$^1/_3$ cup crushed tomatoes in heavy puree

One 1$^1/_{10}$-pound package vacuum-packed potato gnocchi from Italy

1   Bring a large pot of salted water to a boil. Chop sage somewhat coarsely.

2   Melt butter with sage in small skillet over low heat. Add tomatoes and heat through, stirring occasionally, 2 to 3 minutes. Ingredients won't combine completely.

3   Cook gnocchi in boiling water until they rise to surface, 1 to 2 minutes. Drain well. Return them to pot over low heat. Add sauce and heat together, stirring, 15 to 30 seconds. Season with salt and pepper to taste and serve right away.

4 SERVINGS AS A FIRST COURSE

other ideas

SIMPLE TIPS *Good prepared potato gnocchi can be found in the supermarket both frozen and in vacuum packages. Of the brands I've tasted, I prefer the flavor and texture of the vacuum-packed ones from Italy. Look for them in the rice section or ask, as sometimes they're put in an unexpected place.*

Stir and lift the gnocchi with a slotted spoon a few times while they cook to separate any that stick together.

VARIATION *Substitute 2 or 3 whole dried sage leaves, crumbled, for the fresh.*

Polenta with Cheese and Walnuts

Steaming hot polenta is welcomed at the Italian dinner table much in the same way mashed potatoes are here. Polenta, though, starts out as golden cornmeal simmered in water until the grains soften and swell into a soft, mild, and creamy mass. It's a gloriously humble dish, frankly irresistible alongside heartwarming food such as Chicken Cacciatore (page 96), Pork Chops Braised with Marsala (page 136), and even the simplest roast chicken. But basic polenta is often gussied up a bit, too, with tender chopped vegetables or a sprinkle of cheese. This polenta is in that category. It's dressed up with Muenster and Parmesan cheeses, which melt on contact with the heat, and scattered with crunchy walnuts.

2^1/$_2$ tablespoons chopped walnuts
^{2}/$_3$ cup "five-minute polenta"
^{1}/$_2$ cup shredded Muenster cheese (2^1/$_2$ ounces)
3 tablespoons grated Parmesan cheese

1 Preheat oven to 350°F (or use a toaster oven). Toast walnuts on small tray until

golden, about 8 minutes. Bring 2³/₄ cups water almost to a boil in a large saucepan over medium heat and salt to taste.

2 Gradually sprinkle polenta over water, stirring constantly. When all is added, reduce heat to low. Cook, stirring frequently, until thick, smooth, and makes soft mounds in pan, about 5 minutes.

3 Spoon half of the polenta onto warm platter. Scatter with half of Muenster, then half of Parmesan. Cover with remaining polenta, then remaining cheeses over top. Season with pepper and sprinkle with nuts. Serve right away.

4 TO 6 SERVINGS

other ideas

SIMPLE TIPS *A surefire way of keeping the polenta lump-free is to pour the grains right from their measuring cup through a large-meshed handstrainer held directly above the water. Keep stirring the grains as they fall into the pot.*

If there are still some lumps, mash them with a potato masher.

If the water-to-cornmeal ratio for your brand of polenta is different and the polenta is too thick, thin it with tablespoons of hot water. But add them gradually.

Have the Muenster and Parmesan at room temperature so they melt easily.

VARIATIONS *For a more powerful taste, use 3 to 4 tablespoons crumbled Italian Gorgonzola, or to taste, instead of Muenster and Parmesan.*

For a meatless dinner, serve the polenta with a side dish of cooked frozen artichoke hearts and green peas tossed together in butter, along with an arugula or mesclun salad.

Polenta with Zia Pia's Salami Sauce

This delicious polenta dish comes from my friends' Aunt Pia, one of the best cooks in their family. It has all the comforting quality that polenta offers plus earthy salami. The salami, sliced, is browned very quickly in a hot skillet without any oil since it provides its own. Red wine goes in for the last minute and in that brief moment, the salami fills the wine with deep rustic flavor. Then all of it is poured over the polenta. The salami garnishes the mound of soft, yielding yellow grains while some of the wine seeps in and the rest makes a burgundy-colored pool all around.

1 small dry Italian salami (1$\frac{1}{2}$ inches in diameter)
$\frac{2}{3}$ cup "five-minute polenta"
$\frac{1}{4}$ cup red wine
1$\frac{1}{2}$ tablespoons grated Parmesan cheese

1 Peel casing from salami. Cut 16 slices each about $\frac{1}{8}$ inch thick. Refrigerate remaining. Bring 2$\frac{3}{4}$ cups water almost to a boil in a large saucepan over medium heat and salt to taste.

2   Gradually sprinkle polenta over water, stirring constantly (see Simple Tips, page 63). When all is added, reduce heat to low. Cook, stirring frequently, until thick, smooth, and makes soft mounds in pan, about 5 minutes.

3   Spoon polenta onto warm platter. Heat a small dry skillet over medium-high heat. When hot, add salami and brown bottom edges slightly, about 30 seconds. Turn slices, then add wine. Reduce wine to 3 tablespoons, about 60 seconds. Pour salami and wine over polenta. Sprinkle with grated Parmesan and serve right away.

4 TO 5 SERVINGS

other ideas

SIMPLE TIPS *If you're buying the salami at a deli counter, it might help to know that sliced it weighs about 1½ ounces.*

The skillet is hot enough when a few drops of water sizzle and evaporate immediately.

Keep the polenta warm in a low oven while you make the salami sauce.

VARIATION *Aunt Pia topped her polenta with shredded Muenster cheese, then slipped it under the broiler for a minute to melt. Then she poured the salami sauce on top and served it.*

Golden Garlic and Cabbage Risotto

You can make quite a lovely risotto without having to stand at the stove for 20 minutes or so slowly stirring hot broth into rice. In this version, all that's required is a quick initial stir, then about 10 minutes of simmering. The rice will be pleasantly al dente when done and still slightly soupy with broth. When you stir in a generous amount of grated Parmesan, it becomes lusciously creamy like traditional risotto.

1 small head Savoy or green cabbage
3 garlic cloves
$1/4$ cup butter
1 cup Italian arborio rice
$3 1/4$ cups chicken broth
$1/2$ cup grated Parmesan cheese

1   Cut cabbage in half and remove core. Thinly slice enough to measure 2 packed cups. Chop garlic. Melt butter in large saucepan. Add garlic and cook until light gold, stirring frequently, 3 to 4 minutes. Add cabbage and rice. Cook until cabbage begins to wilt, stirring frequently, about 2 minutes.

2   Increase heat to high and gradually stir in broth. Bring to a simmer, stirring occasionally. Reduce heat to low and cover.

3 Cook until slightly al dente, 10 to 11 minutes. Rice should be slightly soupy. Remove saucepan from heat, stir in grated cheese, cover, and let sit 1 minute. Serve right away with grinds of pepper over the top.

4 TO 5 SERVINGS AS A FIRST COURSE

other ideas

SIMPLE TIPS *A 3- to 3 1/2-quart saucepan is the perfect size to make the risotto.*

If the rice has absorbed all the broth when it's done, stir in a little hot *broth to make it somewhat soupy. Then stir in the grated cheese.*

VARIATION *For a beautiful golden-orange-colored risotto, substitute 1 shredded medium carrot for the cabbage. Or use about 2/3 cup frozen and defrosted chopped spinach that has been squeezed to remove the water, 2 to 3 small zucchini sautéed separately first, or about 1/2 pound thin asparagus, trimmed of woody ends, then cut into small pieces.*

Quick Risotto with Tuna and Tomatoes

Based on a recipe from friend and cookbook author Lora Brody, this version using my quick risotto method does not include Parmesan cheese, respecting the Italian rule of not serving cheese with fish. But since arborio rice has a lot more starch than regular long-grain rice, the risotto's "sauce" will still have the creamy body that is the hallmark of risotto, in this case helped by the addition of rich olive oil. The secret to this dish is tuna packed in olive oil, not vegetable oil, or water.

1 large ripe tomato

1 large garlic clove

One 6-ounce can solid light tuna in olive oil

2 tablespoons extra-virgin olive oil

1 cup Italian arborio rice

2 cups bottled clam juice

1   Cut tomato in half and squeeze out and discard seeds. Cut into $1/2$-inch dice. Chop garlic. Drain tuna, reserving oil. Flake tuna with a fork and set aside. Heat oil from tuna with extra-virgin olive oil in a 3- to $3^1/2$-quart saucepan over medium heat. Add garlic and cook until fragrant, stirring frequently, about 1 minute.

2   Add rice and cook, stirring frequently, until it starts to look white, 2 to 3 minutes.

Increase heat to high and gradually stir in clam juice and $1^{1}/_{2}$ cups water. Bring to a simmer, stirring occasionally so rice doesn't stick to bottom of pot. Reduce heat to low and cover.

3 Cook until barely al dente, about 11 minutes. Stir in tuna and tomato and cook, uncovered, stirring frequently, until they heat through, 1 to 2 minutes. Serve hot with grinds of pepper over top.

MAKES 4 TO 5 SERVINGS AS A FIRST COURSE

other ideas

SIMPLE TIPS *It used to be that the only tuna packed in olive oil available in our markets was from Italy, the Progresso brand usually. Now wonderful tuna from Spain can sometimes be found as well as a domestic version or two. Choose from any of them; just be sure the label says "solid light" meat (not white) packed in olive oil. Of course you can always find imported canned tuna at your local Italian delicatessen, too.*

Arborio is just one of the varieties of short-grain, risotto-type rice. It's the kind most frequently sold in markets because it is exported in such quantity. Carnaroli and vialone nano, however, are two other varieties that make a superb risotto. They're available in some supermarkets and at specialty grocers. As with all risotto-type rices, they are pricey.

VARIATIONS *White wine is often used in risottos for some of the liquid. If you like, substitute $^{1}/_{2}$ cup dry white wine for $^{1}/_{2}$ cup broth.*

For a lusty version of this tuna risotto, make risotto puttanesca*: Add 4 chopped anchovy fillets to the olive oil with the garlic in the recipe. Then cook the rice as described. Meanwhile, chop $^{1}/_{3}$ cup pitted black Mediterranean olives and mix with 2 tablespoons* capers (coarsely chopped, too, if large). When the risotto's ready, stir in the olives and capers along with the tuna and tomato.

Top each serving of either the tuna and tomato or risotto puttanesca with a tablespoon of chopped fresh basil.

the simpler the better Seafood

Steamed Clams with Garlic and Olive Oil — 72

Cod Fillets with Roasted Sweet Peppers — 74

Crisp Crusted Flounder — 76

Mussels Steamed with Tomatoes and Vegetables — 78

Oven-Roasted Sea Scallops with Capers and White Wine — 80

Shrimp with Anchovy Butter — 82

Shrimp with Garlic, Onion, and Tomato — 84

Sole with Parmesan Glaze — 86

Roman Swordfish — 88

Sautéed Tuna with Crisp Garlic and Black Olives — 90

Sautéed Bass with Fresh Tomatoes and Basil — 92

Steamed Clams with Garlic and Olive Oil

Sometimes there's nothing more satisfying than traditional tastes. Like these fresh briny clams steamed in white wine with lots of good olive oil and plentiful garlic, sautéed until golden for extra flavor.

4 dozen Littleneck clams or 4 1/2 pounds Manila clams

2/3 cup extra-virgin olive oil

4 large garlic cloves, chopped

1/2 cup white wine

3 tablespoons chopped parsley

1 Rinse clams well under cold running water. Drain.

2 Place olive oil in a pot about twice the volume of clams (or divide between two) over low heat. Add garlic and cook, stirring frequently, until light gold, 2 to 3 minutes. Add wine. Add clams, cover, and increase heat to high. Cook, stirring occasionally, just until clams open, 4 to 5 minutes.

3 Divide clams among bowls. Season broth with pepper to taste; there should be sufficient salt. Ladle over clams and sprinkle with parsley. Serve right away.

4 SERVINGS

SIMPLE TIPS *To ensure the clams are not gritty, soak them in a brine solution of ¹/₃ cup salt to 1 gallon cold water for up to 30 minutes, if you want. Then rinse well and cook.*

Remove the clams as soon as they open; longer cooking will toughen them.

Littleneck clams have a naturally high salt content, Manila clams considerably less so. If the finished Littleneck broth is salty, add a little water. Or season the finished Manila broth with salt, if you like.

SERVING SUGGESTIONS *A tossed salad with fresh or sun-dried tomatoes, or grilled fennel and summer squash. Herb or onion focaccia or crusty bread for dunking.*

VARIATIONS *Add about ¹/₂ cup chopped or crushed canned tomatoes to the garlic after it has turned golden.*

Serve the clams with their broth over spaghetti, linguine, or other cooked pasta.

Cod Fillets with Roasted Sweet Peppers

Here's the plan: Start by roasting sweet peppers and red onions to create a sweet and savory bed of vegetables. Then top the combo with fresh cod fillets and olives for a quick race to the finish line. I prefer using only red peppers, but a combination of red, yellow, and orange peppers makes the dish especially festive looking. Green peppers are a little bitter when roasted, so I leave them out.

3 large red bell peppers

1 medium red onion

3 tablespoons extra-virgin olive oil

$1/3$ cup chopped pitted Kalamata olives

4 cod fillets, 6 to 7 ounces each and about $3/4$ inch thick

2 tablespoons chopped fresh marjoram or parsley

1   Preheat oven to 450°F with rack in top third. Seed and de-rib peppers, then slice into $1/4$-inch-wide strips. Thinly slice red onion. Toss red peppers and onion with 2 tablespoons olive oil in 15 × 10-inch baking dish. Season with salt and pepper.

2   Bake vegetables, stirring occasionally, until almost tender, about 25 minutes. Stir in olives. Set cod on top of vegetables. Drizzle with remaining 1 tablespoon oil and sea-

son with salt and pepper to taste. Bake until cod is barely opaque when a part is separated with tip of knife, 10 to 12 minutes.

3   Sprinkle all with marjoram. Bring baking dish to table and serve right away from dish.

4 SERVINGS

other ideas

SERVING SUGGESTIONS *A tomato and cucumber salad dressed with red wine vinegar and olive oil with a sprinkle of dried oregano. Crusty Italian bread or Little New Potatoes with Lemon Zest, page 196.*

VARIATIONS *Substitute other members of the cod family such as haddock, scrod, or pollock. Or use tilefish or tilapia.*

Add potatoes to the dish for a 1-dish meal: Slice 2 medium red-skinned potatoes into $1/8$-inch-thick rounds, then toss with 1 tablespoon extra-virgin olive oil. Roast them in the baking dish for 10 minutes before the vegetables go in, turning them over once in a while. Now add the peppers and red onion and follow the recipe directions above.

Crisp Crusted Flounder

Kids will like these golden, crisp fish fillets. Because flounder is often so thin, it can overcook easily. The best trick I know to avoid that problem is to fold it in half to make double-thick portions, which makes it easier to handle both before and after the oven.

4 flounder fillets, about 5 ounces each
$1/2$ cup plain, dried bread crumbs
1 large garlic clove, crushed through a press
$1/2$ teaspoon dried oregano
3 tablespoons extra-virgin olive oil
Lemon wedges

1 Preheat oven to 400°F with rack in top third. Lightly oil a 13 × 9-inch glass or metal baking dish. Season fillets with salt and pepper to taste. Fold each fillet in half cross-wise so it forms a triangle of double thickness. Place in one layer in prepared dish.

2 Mix bread crumbs, garlic, and oregano in small bowl. Mix in enough olive oil to make a paste, about $1^1/2$ tablespoons. Spread a thin layer of the crumb mixture over the top of each fillet. Drizzle with remaining olive oil.

3 Bake until topping is lightly browned and crisp, 10 to 12 minutes. Serve right away with lemon wedges on the side.

4 SERVINGS

other ideas

SIMPLE TIP *If the reverse is true and your flounder fillets are thick, do this: Buy two 9- to 10-ounce fillets and cut each one in half crosswise to make 4 servings. They will take a few minutes longer in the oven to cook through.*

SERVING SUGGESTIONS *A raw shredded carrot salad dressed with a garlicky vinegar and oil dressing or Sautéed Asparagus with Onion and Mint (page 174). Because of the bread-crumb coating, you won't need a starch.*

VARIATION *Add a tablespoon of chopped fresh parsley or basil to the bread crumbs, garlic, and oregano.*

Mussels Steamed with Tomatoes and Vegetables

A generous amount of onion, celery, and garlic is heaped into a mound, then finely chopped together to combine the flavors. Then they're cooked with tomatoes. And when the beautiful black bivalves are cooked in this mix, their shells open and they contribute their oceanic juices. The result is a deliciously heady brew for dunking the tender mussel meat.

1 small to medium onion, chopped

1 large celery stalk, chopped

3 large garlic cloves, chopped

4 pounds mussels

$1/4$ cup extra-virgin olive oil

1 cup crushed tomatoes in heavy puree

1   Place onion, celery, and garlic in a mound. Chop together finely. Rinse mussels under cold running water or scrub with a brush if necessary. Drain well.

2   Place olive oil in a pot about twice the volume of mussels (or divide between two) over medium-high heat. Add vegetables and cook until lightly browned and tender-crunchy, stirring occasionally, 6 to 8 minutes. Add tomatoes and $1/2$ cup water. Add

mussels, cover, and cook about 5 minutes or just until they open, transferring them to a large bowl as they're done. Continue to cook remaining, discarding any that do not open.

3 Divide mussels into serving bowls. Season broth with pepper to taste; it should have sufficient salt. Ladle over mussels and serve right away.

4 SERVINGS

other ideas

SIMPLE TIPS *The fibrous material that extrudes from one side of the mussel shell is called a beard, though not all mussels will still have it attached when you buy them. If yours do, snip it off with scissors just before cooking. Doing it earlier will kill them and they must be alive when cooked.*

Stir the mussels up from the bottom of the pot occasionally as they cook because the bottom ones will likely be done first.

Set the serving bowls on a cookie sheet in a low oven as you steam the mussels. Divide the cooked ones among the bowls as they come out of the pot while the rest are finishing. All that's needed is broth over the top before serving.

SERVING SUGGESTIONS *A tossed salad with arugula and plenty of crusty bread for sopping up the broth.*

DRESS IT UP *Sprinkle each bowlful of mussels with grated lemon zest when serving.*

Oven-Roasted Sea Scallops with Capers and White Wine

Big, fat, succulent sea scallops are roasted in a hot oven for mere minutes so their texture stays silken. When served, they're lightly dressed in wine and rosemary-scented pan juices and dotted with just enough salty capers to give their sweet, almost musky taste a bit of an edge.

1 3/4 pounds large sea scallops
3 tablespoons extra-virgin olive oil
Two 3-inch sprigs fresh rosemary or 1 teaspoon dried
1 tablespoon capers
3 tablespoons white wine

1   Preheat oven to 450°F with rack in top third. Choose an ovenproof pan large enough to hold scallops with 1 to 2 inches of space between each. Preheat pan on rack 10 minutes.

2   Peel off tiny side muscle from scallops, if there, and discard. Rinse and dry well on paper towels. Toss in 1 tablespoon of olive oil in large bowl with rosemary. Season with salt and pepper to taste. Lightly chop capers. Combine wine, capers, and remaining 2 tablespoons oil in small bowl. Season lightly with salt and pepper and set aside.

3 Pour scallops and rosemary from bowl onto preheated pan. Turn scallops, where necessary, so each sits flat and separated from one another. Roast until bottoms brown, about 5 minutes. Turn and roast 1 minute more. Pour wine mixture into pan. Cook 30 seconds more or until scallop sides feel slightly springy when lightly squeezed. Remove from oven. Discard rosemary sprigs and serve scallops hot with pan juices.

4 SERVINGS

other ideas

SIMPLE TIPS *The key to browning the scallops is a hot oven, a preheated heavyweight pan such as cast iron or Calphalon, and space between the scallops so they don't steam. All is not lost if the scallops don't brown, however; they will still taste good.*

The wine mixture should bubble up and reduce slightly on contact with the hot pan at the end. If the juices are still a little watery, first remove the scallops to a platter. Then set the pan directly over medium heat for a few seconds to intensify flavor.

SERVING SUGGESTIONS *Swiss chard, sautéed cabbage with a little cream, or Green Beans with Radicchio (page 182). Garlic bread or rice with mushrooms and chopped parsley.*

Shrimp with Anchovy Butter

Shrimp is one of the best friends a busy cook can have; it's available everywhere, almost everyone loves it, and it cooks practically in the blink of an eye. In fact, it *has to* be cooked quickly or its crunchy-tender charm will turn tough and unappetizing. In this recipe, the combination of sweet shrimp, pungent anchovies, and tart lemon is a memorable one.

4 anchovy fillets in oil

1 large garlic clove

1¼ pounds medium shrimp, peeled and deveined

8 tablespoons (1 stick) butter

2 teaspoons fresh lemon juice, plus more to taste

1   Drain anchovy fillets, then chop. Mince garlic clove. Dry shrimp on paper towels.

2   Heat 1 tablespoon butter in skillet over medium-high heat. Add shrimp and cook, stirring frequently, until almost white throughout, 2 to 3 minutes. Do not overcook. Transfer to bowl and cover loosely with foil.

3   Add the remaining 7 tablespoons butter, anchovies, and garlic to skillet and cook over medium-low heat, stirring often, until garlic is light gold and anchovies "dissolve" into sauce, about 1 minute. Stir in 2 teaspoons lemon juice or to taste.

Return shrimp to skillet and heat through gently, 30 seconds. Season with salt and pepper to taste. Serve right away.

4 SERVINGS

SIMPLE TIPS *Be careful when adding salt to the dish since the anchovies are salty to begin with and if you have used salted butter, it has added salt, too.*

Often just-cooked shrimp throws off lots of liquid. In case yours does, set a colander in the bowl to which you are transferring the cooked shrimp. This way you can avoid adding the liquid to the sauce and diluting it.

SERVING SUGGESTIONS *Serve a simple butter lettuce salad tossed with oil and vinegar alongside, or as a first course. Or serve Grilled Summer Squash with Parsley and Oregano (page 194). The anchovy butter cries out for something to soak it up, and steamed rice with fresh parsley would do the job.*

VARIATIONS *Adding fresh asparagus lends another level of flavor to the dish. First snap off and discard the woody ends of about $1/2$ pound of spears, then cut them into 1-inch lengths. Cook them in boiling salted water in the skillet until crisp-tender, about 4 minutes. Drain well and dry on paper towels. Wipe out the skillet, then cook the shrimp according to the recipe. Return the asparagus to skillet with the shrimp at the end.*

Grill the shrimp instead of sautéing them. Slide them onto skewers, season with salt and pepper, and brush them with a little oil. Make the anchovy butter in a little pan on the grill or stovetop and combine them together. Or drizzle them with some sauce and serve the rest on the side.

Shrimp with Garlic, Onion, and Tomato

Many an Italian recipe starts with the cooking of a *battuto,* which is a small slew of chopped vegetables such as celery, carrot, onion, garlic, parsley, and tomato and sometimes bits of pancetta, ham, or simply ham fat. The *battuto* gives the dish foundation and flavor, but even using a few of these elements such as the onion, parsley, and garlic here can really make the dish. Yes, tomato shows up, too, but in diced form at the end when the shrimp are practically done. Heated for only a minute or two, the fresh tomatoes keep their integrity but the juices flow and create a light, moist sauce.

1 medium to large tomato

$1/2$ small onion, thinly sliced

2 large garlic cloves, sliced

$1/2$ cup flat-leaf parsley leaves

$13/4$ pounds medium shrimp, peeled and deveined

$1/3$ cup extra-virgin olive oil

1   Cut tomato into small dice to measure 1 cup and set aside. Make mound of onion, garlic, and parsley, and chop together finely. Dry shrimp on paper towels.

2. Place olive oil in large skillet over low heat. Add chopped vegetables and cook until tender and garlic is light gold, stirring occasionally, about 10 minutes.

3. Stir in shrimp still over low heat. Turn pieces when mostly pink on bottom side, about 1 minute. Cook until almost done, about 1 minute more. Stir in tomato and cook just until juices flow and shrimp are white throughout, 1 to 2 minutes. Remove skillet from heat and season with salt to taste and generously with pepper. Serve hot.

4 SERVINGS

other ideas

SIMPLE TIPS *If you buy frozen, already cleaned medium shrimp, figure 10 to 12 pieces per person.*

Drying shrimp on paper towels before cooking makes a difference, particularly when the shrimp have been defrosted and are wet. Without drying, they will stick to the pan or dilute the sauce, or both.

If the sauce is watery when the shrimp are done, remove the shrimp to a bowl with a slotted spoon and boil it down until slightly thickened. The pieces of tomato may break down but the flavor will have intensified. Be sure to season the sauce after it has reduced in volume, though.

SERVING SUGGESTIONS *An arugula or tossed salad with shaved strips of Parmesan or Romano cheese and raw fennel or peeled broccoli stems cut in slivers, if you like. Buttered orzo, steamed rice, or crisp, warm Italian bread.*

Sole with Parmesan Glaze

When you find fresh lemon, gray, or petrale sole in the market, pounce. They are similar to flounder, but with more depth of sweet, subtle flavor. All that's needed is to enhance their delicate taste, not mask it. So keep any other ingredients simple and few. Many Italians would shudder at the thought of using cheese when cooking fish, but breaking the rules sometimes pays off. The combination can be very good, as in this easy dish.

1 tablespoon extra-virgin olive oil
4 sole fillets, 7 ounces each
$1/3$ cup all-purpose flour
4 tablespoons freshly grated Parmesan cheese
Lemon wedges

1   Preheat broiler with rack placed 6 inches from heat source. Heat olive oil in large nonstick skillet over medium-high heat.

2   Season fillets with salt and pepper to taste. Fold each fillet in half crosswise to make a triangular shaped, double-thick fillet. Lightly dredge fillets in flour, patting off excess. Place in skillet and reduce heat to medium. Cook until undersides of fish are

golden brown, about 3 minutes. Turn and cook until fish is barely opaque when opened at a natural separation with tip of a knife, about 4 minutes.

3 Sprinkle 1 tablespoon grated cheese evenly over top of each fillet. Slide pan under broiler just until cheese melts, about 1 minute. Serve right away, with lemon wedges on side.

4 SERVINGS

other ideas

SERVING SUGGESTIONS *Swiss chard, escarole, or Savoy cabbage sautéed with a little garlic in olive oil or Leeks Baked with Butter and Marjoram (page 186). Little New Potatoes with Lemon Zest (page 196) are lovely with this.*

VARIATION *Just before placing the skillet under the broiler, add 4 tablespoons butter to the pan. It will melt as the fish broils. Serve the fish drizzled with the melted butter.*

Roman Swordfish

Romans are big admirers of swordfish, or *pescespada,* as it's known. As they will say, the best way to appreciate such a delicately meaty fish is to cook it as simply as possible. In this version, the steaks are briefly marinated in garlic, olive oil, vinegar, and a dash of crushed red pepper flakes. Then they're baked just long enough to cook through so they retain their creamy texture.

1/4 cup extra-virgin olive oil

2 tablespoons red wine vinegar

Pinch crushed red pepper flakes

1 large garlic clove

4 swordfish steaks, 7 ounces each and 1 inch thick

1   Combine olive oil and vinegar in a small bowl. Stir in pepper flakes, 1/4 teaspoon pepper, and salt to taste. Cut garlic in half lengthwise. Rub garlic over both sides of swordfish, then crush halves lightly with a knife. Add garlic to bowl.

2   Preheat oven to 425°F. Lay swordfish in baking pan large enough to allow 1 to 2 inches between each. Pour half the marinade over swordfish and set rest aside. Turn swordfish to coat, then cover loosely. Let sit at room temperature 15 to 45 minutes.

3 Bake swordfish without turning until just cooked through, about 20 minutes. Transfer to platter with pan juices and spoon remaining marinade over fish.

4 SERVINGS

other ideas

SERVING SUGGESTIONS *Tossed salad with arugula, parsley leaves, and Bibb lettuce, or Sautéed Asparagus with Onion and Mint (page 174). Boiled little new potatoes sprinkled with oregano or Arborio Rice Pilaf with Porcini Mushrooms (page 200).*

DRESS IT UP *Cut a beautifully ripe tomato into small dice and scatter over the top of the swordfish. Then drizzle with the second half of the marinade.*

Sautéed Tuna with Crisp Garlic and Black Olives

These tuna steaks are quickly cooked in olive oil with fine slivers of garlic and meaty whole olives. When the steaks are done, the garlic is slightly crisp and chewy and the oil is infused with its flavor and a little vinegar to highlight the tastes. They're served in a small pool of the flavorful oil with the olives and garlic scattered over top. A sprinkle of parsley brings a little bit of freshness to the richness of the rest.

4 large garlic cloves

4 tuna steaks, 6 ounces each and $1/2$ to $3/4$ inch thick

$1/2$ cup extra-virgin olive oil

Flour for dusting

16 dry-cured black olives, pitted

2 tablespoons red wine vinegar

$1 1/2$ tablespoons coarsely chopped parsley

1 Very thinly slice garlic lengthwise. Dry tuna steaks on paper towels and season to taste with salt and pepper. Heat olive oil in large skillet over medium-high heat. While oil heats lightly dredge tuna steaks in flour, patting off excess.

2 Brown first side of tuna steaks until light gold, about 2 minutes. Turn and reduce heat to low. First scatter olives, then garlic around fish. Cook 1 minute more for pink or 2 to 3 minutes more for well done. Transfer fish to platter or plates. Immediately add vinegar to skillet and cook over low heat 1 minute. Remove from heat and season with salt and pepper to taste.

3 Spoon sauce over fish. Sprinkle with parsley and serve hot.

4 SERVINGS

other ideas

SIMPLE TIPS *Try not to be tempted to buy tuna steaks more than $3/4$ inch thick. In this dish, the tuna stays tender and tastes best when each bite has the right proportion of meat to garlic, olives, and olive oil. If the market has only thick steaks, you can—or ask the fishmonger to—cut them in half horizontally.*

The garlic should not become more than light gold in color or it will taste burned. If the tuna is not done when the garlic is done, then pull the pan off the heat, remove the garlic, and add it back to the sauce at the end.

SERVING SUGGESTIONS *Steamed broccoli or sautéed broccoli rabe, whole or sliced roasted eggplant, or Summer Sweet Pepper, Tomato, and Onion Salad with Basil (page 162). Crisped, warm Italian bread, white rice, or Little New Potatoes with Lemon Zest (page 196).*

Sautéed Bass with Fresh Tomatoes and Basil

During the summer, when tomatoes and basil are sharing the peak of the glorious season, we want to be outside too and not spending a lot of time in a hot kitchen! So, here's a lovely light dish that calls for very little time behind the stove and still makes praiseworthy results. The heart of the dish is in the juicy flavor and fresh texture of the tomatoes. Which is why in this recipe they don't get cooked but, instead, are tossed in warm garlicky olive oil to bring out their sun-filled taste.

2 large ripe tomatoes

1 large garlic clove

4 tablespoons extra-virgin olive oil

4 sea bass fillets, 6 to 7 ounces each

3 tablespoons fresh basil

1 Seed tomatoes and cut into $1/2$-inch dice. Mince garlic. Heat 1 tablespoon olive oil in large nonstick skillet over medium-high heat until very hot but not smoking. Dry fillets with paper towels, then season with salt and pepper to taste. Place in skillet, skin side up, until underside is lightly browned, about 3 minutes. Turn and cook until fish is just white throughout when pushed open with the tip of a sharp knife, 3 to 4 minutes. Transfer to a platter and cover loosely with foil to keep warm.

2 Place tomatoes in a medium bowl. Heat garlic and remaining 3 tablespoons olive oil in small skillet over low heat just until garlic is beginning to soften, about 30 seconds. Pour over tomatoes in bowl and toss gently. Season with salt and pepper to taste.

3 Spoon tomatoes and oil over fish. Tear basil into small pieces and scatter over fillets. Serve right away.

4 SERVINGS

other ideas

SIMPLE TIPS *Peeling and seeding a tomato is quick. Bring a medium pot of water to a boil. Make a shallow "x" in the end of the tomato opposite the stem. Then slip the toma-to into the boiling water for 10 seconds only and remove it. Start peeling off the skin from the "x" with a paring knife. Once peeled, cut it in half crosswise and gently squeeze out the seeds from each half. Then you can dice or cut it any way you like.*

Very hot oil in a very hot skillet is crucial to successfully sautéing fish fillets. To check if the pan and oil are hot enough, sprinkle a pinch of flour into the skillet. It should immediately sizzle and begin to brown. And be sure not to overcrowd the fillets or they will steam and start to stick instead of brown.

To keep the fillets from sticking to the pan, by far the easiest way is to use a nonstick skillet (of course, still cooking over proper heat). Heavy-gauge skillets with thick bottoms work best. Also, to help turn the fillets, use a thin metal spatula that you can easily slip under the delicate fish.

To help keep the tomato-garlic oil warm as you toss the mixture, warm the bowl first. But don't make it hot or you might cook the tomatoes.

SERVING SUGGESTIONS *Cooked couscous, angel hair pasta, or orzo, lightly dressed with olive oil and lemon zest.*

VARIATIONS *Use a variety of color tomatoes if they're available: orange, golden yellow, or any heirloom-type varieties. They add more color and wonderful taste. Or use about 1½ pints multicolored cherry or grape tomatoes. Simply cut each in half and don't worry about the seeds.*

Other delicate white-fleshed fillets such as red snapper, halibut, or a firm type sole such as East Coast gray sole or West Coast petrale would also be delicious. Or bake fillets of cod and spoon the tomatoes over them when they come out of the oven.

Turn it into a grill dinner and cook shrimp, salmon, or trout on the grill. Spoon the tomatoes over the cooked fillets just as in the recipe.

the simpler the better Chicken and Turkey

Chicken Cacciatore   96

Chicken Diavolo   98

Chicken Breasts in Lemon and Egg Sauce   100

Chicken Cutlets in Garlic Cream   102

Chicken Fricassea with Capers   104

Chicken Marsala with Mushrooms   106

Chicken Breasts with Pancetta and Sage   108

Chicken Valdostana   110

Roast Chicken Legs with Balsamic Vinegar and Tomato   112

Chicken with Rosemary Sauce   114

Turkey Piccata with Mozzarella   116

Roast Turkey Breast with Potatoes, Marjoram, and Sage   118

Chicken Cacciatore

An old favorite never loses its appeal, and that counts for chicken cacciatore. Traditionally made with cut-up pieces of chicken cooked with mushrooms, tomatoes, garlic, and onion, this one calls for only thighs. It has all the earthy goodness of the original with one small addition: half a bouillon cube crumbled into the pot for better flavor, just like Zia Emma, my friend Marie's aunt Emma, always used.

2 1/2 to 3 pounds chicken thighs (8 pieces)
1 small onion, chopped
2 large garlic cloves, chopped
1/2 pound white button mushrooms, coarsely chopped
1 1/4 cups drained and coarsely chopped canned tomatoes
1/2 beef boullion cube

1   Dry thighs on paper towels. Season with salt and pepper. Heat a large, deep skillet over high heat without oil. Doing in 2 batches, add thighs skin side down and brown until golden, 3 to 5 minutes. Turn and lightly brown other side, about 1 minute. Remove to platter as done. Pour off all but 2 tablespoons rendered fat.

2   Reduce heat to medium. Stir in onion and garlic. Stir in mushrooms. Cook, stirring occasionally, until vegetables begin to soften and brown, about 5 minutes. Add

tomatoes. Crumble in boullion cube. Return thighs and cover. Reduce heat to low. Simmer until thighs are tender when pierced with fork, 25 to 30 minutes.

3   Transfer thighs to platter. Boil down juices over medium heat until lightly thickened, 2 to 3 minutes, stirring occasionally. Season with salt and pepper and pour over thighs. Serve hot.

4 SERVINGS

other ideas

SIMPLE TIPS *A Dutch oven or stew pot works, too. Whichever pan you choose, the thighs cook best in a single layer with a little space between each piece.*

The skin renders enough of its own fat to brown the thighs without adding oil and without sticking. Be sure the pan is good and hot when you add the thighs, though, so the fat starts to render right away. If the first piece doesn't sizzle immediately, remove it and heat the pan a little longer.

SERVING SUGGESTIONS *Raw fennel and beet salad or cooked Swiss chard. Buttered rice or pasta, or soft polenta with shredded Muenster cheese on top.*

VARIATION *Use mixed chicken pieces instead of thighs. Cut the breasts in half cross-wise, if you like, so there's more white meat to go around.*

Chicken Diavolo

The original of this dish is made with a whole chicken, flattened, marinated, then grilled over a wood fire. Delicious for sure. But a simplified version with quick-cooking chicken breasts can be good too, whether cooked over charcoal or in a ridged grill pan on top of the stove as they're done here. The devil in the dish, the diavolo, performs his work in simple yet effective fashion: crushed black peppercorns pressed onto the breast. His marinating cohorts, fresh lemon juice and olive oil, offer a speck of relief to his heat.

2 teaspoons whole black peppercorns

Four 7- to 8-ounce skinless, boneless chicken breasts

2 tablespoons freshly squeezed lemon juice

$1/2$ teaspoon grated lemon zest

$1/4$ cup extra-virgin olive oil

1 Place a sheet of plastic wrap on counter with peppercorns in center. Fold over sides and ends to enclose. Crush peppercorns to small pieces with meat mallet. Dry chicken breasts with paper towels. Sprinkle peppercorns evenly over both sides, pressing to adhere.

2 Whisk lemon juice, lemon zest, and olive oil together in large bowl. Season with salt to

taste. Add chicken breasts and turn to coat. Marinate 15 minutes, turning several times.

3 Heat a ridged grill pan over medium heat. Place breasts rounded side down in pan, reserving marinade in bowl. Cook first side until golden, lightly spooning reserved marinade over tops as they cook, 5 to 6 minutes. Lower heat at any point if they brown too quickly. Turn, and cook through, spooning over any remaining marinade, 5 to 6 minutes. Serve hot.

4 SERVINGS

other ideas

SIMPLE TIPS *The peppercorns can also be crushed with a hammer or with the back of a small skillet using a rocking/pressing motion. Or coarsely grind them in a small electric coffee grinder set aside for grinding spices.*

Drying the chicken breasts with paper towels helps the peppercorns and the marinade adhere.

SERVING SUGGESTIONS *Tossed salad with slivered fennel or celery and sliced radishes sprinkled with Gorgonzola cheese. Penne or other short pasta in a light tomato sauce or Italian-Style Potato Salad (page 164).*

DRESS IT UP *Slice the cooked breasts on the diagonal and lay them on a bed of cooked spinach or chard.*

VARIATIONS *Split whole Cornish hens down the back, then flatten them before marinating and grilling them. Or use cut-up pieces of chicken. Large shrimp, lobster tails, or sea scallops can be done diavolo fashion, too.*

Add chopped fresh oregano or a little fresh rosemary to the marinade. Or use dried.

Chicken Breasts in Lemon and Egg Sauce

Big chunks of chicken breast cook gently on top of the stove with butter, a nice amount of onion, and some rosemary. And when they're done, the spoonful of juices in the pan gets thickened with egg yolks blended with lemon juice and it coats the pieces in a creamy, lemony sauce. Most well known with braised lamb, this egg and lemon sauce comes from a region in central Italy called The Marches.

4 skinless, boneless chicken breasts, 7 ounces each
1 medium to large onion
1$^1/_2$ tablespoons butter
$^3/_4$ teaspoon finely chopped fresh rosemary or $^1/_2$ teaspoon dried
2 egg yolks
$^1/_4$ cup fresh lemon juice

1 Dry chicken breasts on paper towels. Cut each into quarters. Finely chop onion.

2 Melt butter in large, deep skillet over medium-low heat. Add onion and cook, stirring occasionally, until light gold, 10 to 12 minutes. Stir in chicken and rosemary and season lightly with salt. Add 1 tablespoon water, bring to simmer, and cover. Cook, stirring occasionally, until just cooked through, 12 to 15 minutes. There should be about 1 tablespoon juices in pan. Remove skillet from heat.

3 Lightly beat yolks with fork and gradually add lemon juice. Reduce heat to very low and return skillet to heat. Gradually stir in egg mixture and cook, stirring, until thickened and coats chicken, 30 to 60 seconds. Immediately remove from heat, then season with salt to taste and generous pepper. Serve hot.

4 SERVINGS

other ideas

SIMPLE TIPS *The chicken cooks best in a pan large enough to hold it in one layer.*

If there's more than a tablespoon of juices in the pan when the chicken is done, transfer the chicken to a bowl and boil down the juices. Reduce the heat to low, return the chicken to the pan, then stir in the yolks mixed with lemon juice.

SERVING SUGGESTIONS *Sliced carrots sautéed slowly in olive oil until tender and lightly browned or Green Beans and Zucchini with Potatoes (page 184). Buttered egg pasta or noodles or potatoes coarsely mashed with milk and butter.*

VARIATION *Replace the rosemary with fresh or dried sage or thyme.*

Chicken Cutlets in Garlic Cream

These cutlets are lightly browned in butter with finely slivered garlic. Then they finish their last minute or two of cooking with a gentle simmer in cream. But before they reach the skillet in the first place, they're sliced in half horizontally to allow more of their surface to drink in the cream. When done, the garlic flavor is mellow and perfumes the dish with nutty taste. A squeeze of fresh lemon at the end creates a quiet balance between these simple elements.

2 large garlic cloves
4 skinless, boneless chicken breasts, 7 ounces each
$1^{1}/_{2}$ tablespoons butter
$^{1}/_{3}$ cup heavy cream
4 lemon wedges

1 Thinly slice garlic lengthwise. Doing one at a time, lay chicken breast flat on counter and slice in half horizontally. Repeat with other breasts to make 8 cutlets total. Dry on paper towels. Season with salt and pepper to taste. Melt butter in a very large nonstick skillet (or use 2 skillets) over medium-high heat.

2 Add garlic and cook, stirring, just until fragrant, about 30 seconds. Add chicken and lightly brown first side, about 1 minute. Turn and reduce heat to medium. Cook 1 minute more. Chicken should lie in a single layer or be no more than slightly overlapping.

3 Pour cream over chicken; it will not completely cover. Cook over low heat at gentle simmer, uncovered, until chicken is just cooked through and cream slightly reduced, about 1 minute. Cream should lightly coat chicken. Transfer chicken to platter with cream and season with another grind or two of pepper. Serve right away with a lemon wedge for each serving.

4 TO 5 SERVINGS

other ideas

SIMPLE TIPS *The garlic should not become more than faintly golden. If necessary, remove it while you finish lightly browning the cutlets, then return it to the pan with the cream.*

Turn the cutlets once or twice during cooking so they cook evenly. Some will probably be thinner than others and will cook faster. If so, transfer those to a platter and cover loosely to keep warm while finishing the rest.

If the cream is a little watery when the cutlets are ready, remove them from the pan and boil it down, stirring, for a few seconds or until it coats a spoon.

SERVING SUGGESTIONS *Green peas, braised or grilled fennel, or Artichoke Hearts with Onion, Balsamic Vinegar, and Parmesan Cheese (page 172). A sliced tomato salad would be good, too, if not serving artichoke hearts. Rice, tiny pasta like ditalini, or Arborio Rice Pilaf with Porcini Mushrooms (page 200).*

DRESS IT UP *Stir 1 or 2 tablespoons Gorgonzola cheese, or to taste, into the cream as soon as the cutlets are out of the pan. Pour the sauce over the cutlets and sprinkle with peeled, seeded, and diced tomatoes and a scattering of fresh basil.*

VARIATIONS *A sprinkle of capers is nice over the top when serving.*
Serve the cutlets on a bed of asparagus spears or lightly wilted spinach.

Chicken Fricassea with Capers

In the United States and in France, a fricassee conjures up the vision of a tender poultry stew, often cooked in wine. Italy has its own too, called a *fricassea*—this one with little briney capers. And there are arguments that the very first fricassea was made by the Romans hundreds of years ago. But what matters right now is dinner! and how good this dish is and how easy to prepare.

1 medium onion

1 medium carrot

1 medium celery stalk

1 tablespoon extra-virgin olive oil

One 4-pound chicken, cut into 8 serving pieces

$1/2$ cup dry white wine

$1 1/2$ teaspoons drained capers

2 tablespoons chopped parsley

1 Chop onion. Cut both carrot and celery into $1/2$-inch dice. Heat olive oil in Dutch oven over medium-high heat. Dry chicken pieces on paper towels, then season with salt and pepper to taste. In batches without crowding, add chicken to pot and cook, turning occasionally, until lightly browned all over, about 6 minutes. Transfer to platter.

2 Pour out all but 2 tablespoons fat. Add onion, carrot, and celery to pot and cover.

Cook, stirring occasionally, until softened, 3 to 5 minutes. Add wine and bring to boil, scraping up browned bits on pot bottom. Stir in $1/2$ cup water. Return chicken to pot, placing dark meat pieces on bottom. Chicken will not be covered with liquid. Cover pot and cook until thigh juices run clear when pierced with a fork or skewer, about 40 minutes.

3   Transfer chicken to a serving dish and loosely cover with aluminum foil. Let cooking liquid stand in pot a few minutes to let fat rise to surface. Skim fat from surface and discard. Stir in capers. Over medium-high heat, reduce liquid by about half, 3 to 4 minutes, or until well flavored. Pour over chicken, sprinkle with parsley, and serve right away.

4 SERVINGS

other ideas

SIMPLE TIP *Since poultry dark meat takes longer to cook than the white meat, arrange the drumsticks, thighs, and wings in the bottom of the pot so they're in direct contact with the cooking liquid. Then with the breasts placed on top, they will cook in the flavorful steam and still be done at the same time as the drumsticks.*

SERVING SUGGESTIONS *Eggplant with Red Onion and Tomato (page 180) and a green salad. Simple steamed rice or Arborio Rice Pilaf with Porcini Mushrooms (page 200).*

VARIATIONS *For a slightly richer result, replace the water with $1/2$ cup chicken broth. After skimming the chicken fat from the cooking liquid, add 2 tablespoons heavy cream and let the pot juices reduce together. This small amount will lend a delicate voluptuousness to the sauce.*

Instead of parsley, use another fresh herb with an Italian accent such as marjoram, rosemary, or basil, or a mixture. Or use an herb not in the Italian repertoire such as dill, tarragon, or chives; the taste will still be delicious.

Chicken Marsala with Mushrooms

Marsala, the sweetish, smoky-tinged wine from Sicily, bathes this tender chicken and meaty mushrooms in a rich syrupy coat during the last minutes of cooking and imparts its memorable flavor. Before cooking, the chicken breasts are thinly sliced like scallopini so they'll cook quickly and stay juicy. In addition, the cutlets are sautéed in butter, which adds a delicately nutty element. Just be sure to keep a close eye on their cooking so the butter doesn't go beyond lightly toasted in color.

$1/2$ pound cremini or white button mushrooms
4 skinless, boneless chicken breasts, 7 ounces each
4 tablespoons butter
Flour for dredging
$2/3$ cup dry Marsala

1   Thinly slice mushrooms. Slice chicken breasts in half horizontally. Dry on paper towels. Melt 1 tablespoon butter in large nonstick skillet over high heat. Cook mushrooms, stirring occasionally, until tender and brown, 5 to 6 minutes. Season lightly with salt and pepper. Transfer to bowl with any pan juices.

2   Season chicken with salt and pepper to taste. Dip in flour and pat off excess. Using

same skillet and doing in 2 batches, melt remaining 3 tablespoons butter over medium to medium-high heat. When butter froths, cook first batch, turning once, until lightly browned on both sides but not quite cooked through, 2 to 4 minutes total. Reduce heat at any time if butter starts to darken. Transfer batches to platter in one layer.

3   Increase heat to high and add Marsala. Boil down to syrupy consistency, 4 to 5 minutes, stirring occasionally. Reduce heat to low and return chicken, mushrooms, and any platter juices to pan. Turn in sauce to coat and heat through, 1 to 2 minutes. Lay chicken on plates and top with mushrooms and any juices left in pan. Serve hot.

4 SERVINGS

other ideas

SIMPLE TIPS *To easily slice a chicken breast, first lay it horizontally in front of you. Place the knife blade at the center part of the thicker end. Slice horizontally until you reach the small end, holding your hand flat on the top the whole time to steady it. Then peel off the top to make 2 pieces.*

Lay the chicken in 1 layer on a platter as you flour them. This helps prevent the flour from turning soggy. And be sure to cook them just as soon as they're floured.

SERVING SUGGESTIONS *Sliced tomatoes with vinegar and olive oil, roasted peppers, or mixed greens with Belgian endive and watercress. Roasted Potatoes or steamed rice.*

DRESS IT UP *Sauté a mixture of mushrooms such as creminis or portobellos, oysters, and shiitakes. Sprinkle the dish with minced fresh chives or oregano.*

VARIATION *Veal, pork, or turkey scallopini make different and good substitutes for the chicken.*

Chicken Breasts with Pancetta and Sage

Boneless chicken breasts are wrapped in thin slices of pancetta, the Italian unsmoked bacon, with sage leaves tucked in between. Then the breasts are slowly sautéed until the pancetta turns beautiful shades of gold and brown and lightly crisp. When you taste it, the chicken is tender and juicy and its mild flavor is punched up by the pronounced taste of sage and the slightly salty pancetta.

4 skinless, boneless chicken breasts, 7 ounces each
8 large fresh sage leaves
8 very thin slices pancetta (6 ounces)
1 tablespoon extra-virgin olive oil

1   Dry chicken on paper towels. Season lightly with pepper (the pancetta supplies the salt). Lay rounded side up. Place 2 leaves of sage, separated by at least 1 inch, on each. Wrap 2 slices of pancetta around each breast with edges next to each other but not overlapping. Press to adhere.

2   Heat olive oil in large skillet over low heat. Add chicken rounded side down and cook until pancetta fat is light gold, 6 to 7 minutes (the pancetta will be darker brown). Turn and cook until golden and brown on the bottom and just cooked through, 6 to 7 minutes.

3 Serve right away.

4 SERVINGS

SIMPLE TIPS *Some pancetta is cured with pepper. Ask the deli counterman if the one you're buying is. If so, the chicken won't need to be seasoned with pepper.*

Wrap the pancetta in a slight diagonal around the breasts; it makes an attractive finished look.

Be sure the pan is hot before adding the breasts so the pancetta doesn't stick.

To turn the breasts, use tongs or slip a spatula underneath and hold the top with the back of a spoon to help keep the pancetta from falling off.

SERVING SUGGESTIONS *Arugula salad, baked acorn squash, or Baked Spinach with Garlic Bread Crumbs (page 192). Crusty Italian bread or soft polenta if not serving the squash.*

DRESS IT UP *Just the tiniest bit of pan juices on top of the chicken make the dish seem a little fancy. To make them, pour off the fat in the pan once the breasts are removed, then add $1/4$ cup water and 2 tablespoons freshly squeezed lemon juice. Reduce them, scraping up the brown bits on the bottom with a wooden spoon, to 2 to 3 flavorful tablespoons. Drizzle over the breasts.*

VARIATION *Replace the fresh sage with $3/4$ teaspoon dried rubbed sage, sprinkling it over the breasts before wrapping them.*

Chicken Valdostana

Fontina, a delicately nutty cheese produced in the north in the Val d'Aosta where Italy borders both France and Switzerland, lends this chicken its name, as well as a good measure of personality. These chicken cutlets are pounded thin, stuffed with cheese and slices of coppa salami for a touch of robust flavor, and breaded. When sautéed they turn out crisp and light and the Fontina melts beautifully inside.

6 small skinless, boneless chicken breasts, about 4 ounces each

4 ounces Italian Fontina d'Aosta cheese, shredded (1 cup)

12 thin slices sweet coppa salami ($^1/_4$ pound)

Flour for dredging

2 eggs

$^1/_3$ cup plus 1 teaspoon extra-virgin olive oil

1 cup plain dry bread crumbs

1   Lay chicken cutlets between sheets of plastic wrap. Pound to an even $^1/_4$-inch thickness with meat mallet or bottom of small skillet; each should measure about 5 x 7 inches. Season with salt and pepper to taste. Sprinkle cheese over tops up to $^1/_2$ inch of edges. Lay 2 slices of salami over cheese, overlapping if necessary. Fold each cutlet in half to form 6 triangular packets with stuffing inside.

2   Preheat oven to 300°F. Place flour on plate. Lightly beat eggs with 2 tablespoons

water and 1 teaspoon olive oil in shallow bowl. Place bread crumbs on plate. Doing one at a time, dredge cutlets in flour. Dip in egg to coat. Finally, coat all over with bread crumbs, pressing in lightly. Lay in single layer on platter and refrigerate 10 to 15 minutes to set breading.

3 Heat half the remaining $1/3$ cup olive oil in very large nonstick skillet over medium heat. Doing in 2 batches, cook each side until golden brown, about 3 minutes a side. Keep warm on paper towel–lined cookie sheet in oven while cooking second batch. Serve hot.

4 TO 6 SERVINGS

other ideas

SIMPLE TIPS *No 4-ounce chicken breasts in the market? Then buy three 8-ounce ones and cut them in half horizontally to make 6 pieces. Or buy thin, precut cutlets. Either way they will still need to be pounded.*

If any of the pounded breasts are a lot larger than others, then cut a piece from a large one, overlap it onto a small one, and gently pound the overlapping edges. The breading will hold them together for cooking.

SERVING SUGGESTIONS *Roasted peppers with olive oil and vinegar or a bitter greens salad. Steamed or grilled asparagus or Green Beans with Radicchio (page 182). Mashed potatoes, if you'd like a starch.*

VARIATIONS *Replace the Fontina with another good melting cheese like Swiss Gruyère or Emmentaler, or use mozzarella, either plain or smoked.*

A slice of prosciutto or boiled ham can be substituted for the salami.

Roast Chicken Legs with Balsamic Vinegar and Tomato

I have seen versions of this recipe where the chicken legs are sautéed in a skillet, but I prefer roasting them because it provides more of the dark, flavorful drippings that add character to the pan juices. Plus you don't have to deal with fat splattering all over the stovetop!

4 chicken drumsticks

4 chicken thighs

1 tablespoon extra-virgin olive oil

1 teaspoon dried oregano

1 large garlic clove, finely chopped

One 28-ounce can chopped tomatoes in juice, drained

$1/4$ cup balsamic vinegar

1 Place rack in center of oven and preheat to 400°F.

2 Toss drumsticks, thighs, olive oil, oregano, and salt and pepper to taste in large bowl to coat. Arrange chicken, skin side up, in 9 x 13-inch metal baking pan. Roast until chicken juices run clear when thigh is pierced with a metal skewer, about 45 minutes. Transfer chicken to platter and cover loosely to keep warm.

3 Pour out all but 1 tablespoon of fat from pan. Place pan over medium heat on stove. Add garlic and cook, stirring frequently, until fragrant, 30 to 60 seconds. Add tomatoes and vinegar, stirring up browned bits on pan bottom. Bring to boil, then simmer until juices are deeply flavorful, 1 to 2 minutes. Season with salt and pepper to taste. Return chicken to pan and turn to coat with juices. Serve right away, with juices spooned on top.

4 SERVINGS

other ideas

SERVING SUGGESTIONS *Peas, cauliflower, or broccoli rabe with garlic. Serve the chicken over fresh pasta like fettuccine or pappardelle. Or simply serve over dried wide egg noodles.*

Chicken with Rosemary Sauce

During my restaurant career, I made this dish countless times for the nightly staff supper. The fact that I still make it for my family and friends is high praise, indeed. Sometimes I just toss everything together in a roasting pan and let it bake, but standing the chicken first does help it reach golden-brown perfection.

1 medium onion

1 medium carrot

1 tablespoon olive oil

One 4-pound chicken, cut into 8 serving pieces

6 fresh rosemary sprigs, each about 3 inches long

2 garlic cloves, chopped

1   Coarsely chop onion and carrot. Mound on chopping board and continue chopping together until finely chopped. Preheat oven to 425°F.

2   Heat oil in 12-inch ovenproof skillet over medium-high heat. Season chicken with $1/2$ teaspoon salt and $1/4$ teaspoon pepper. In batches without crowding, add chicken to skillet, skin side down. Cook until underside is lightly browned, about 3 minutes. Turn and brown the other side, about 3 minutes more. Transfer chicken to platter. Pour off all but 1 tablespoon fat. Return to stove, add onion-carrot mixture to skillet, and reduce heat to medium. Cook, stirring often, until vefetables soften, about 3 minutes.

Add rosemary and garlic and cook, stirring often, until very fragrant, about 1 minute more. Add 1 cup water and scrape up browned bits on bottom of pan. Return chicken to skillet, skin side up.

3   Place skillet in oven and bake until chicken is golden brown and an instant-read thermometer inserted in thickest part of breast reads 170°F, about 35 minutes. Transfer chicken to platter and tent with aluminum foil to keep warm. If the liquid in the skillet has evaporated, stir in $1/2$ cup water. Holding sprigs with tongs, swish rosemary in cooking liquid to release leaves from stems; discard stems. Let cooking liquid stand 3 minutes. Tilt skillet so liquid collects in the corner of the skillet and skim off any clear yellow fat that rises to the top. Taste sauce and season with salt and pepper. Pour sauce over chicken and serve right away.

4 SERVINGS

other ideas

SIMPLE TIP *The skillet size is quite important here, because a pan with a diameter less than 12 inches will be too small to hold the chicken. Be sure that the skillet, handle and all, will fit in the oven. Some kitchenware companies now make 12-inch-wide flameproof metal casseroles, which also work well for this dish.*

SERVING SUGGESTIONS *Serve the chicken with Little New Potatoes with Lemon Zest (page 196), to soak up the sauce, and a simple sautéed green vegetable, such as asparagus, green beans, or broccoli.*

VARIATION *Because of the flavorful, browned chicken juices that collect in the bottom of the pan during sautéing, it isn't necessary to use any liquid other than water to deglaze the skillet. However, if you wish, substitute $1/4$ cup dry white wine for an equal amount of the water.*

Turkey Piccata with Mozzarella

These piccata are tender cutlets from turkey breast sautéed until light golden and doused with lemon juice. And they're good and satisfying just like that. But here, slices of cheese are laid over the cutlets, then run under a hot broiler to melt. The dish becomes good, satisfying, and special when made with milky-fresh mozzarella.

6 ounces fresh mozzarella cheese

Eight 3-ounce turkey cutlets ($1\frac{1}{2}$ pounds total)

Flour for dredging

3 tablespoons olive oil

3 tablespoons freshly squeezed lemon juice

1   Preheat broiler with rack 3 to 4 inches away. Cut mozzarella into eight $\frac{1}{4}$-inch-thick slices. Dry turkey cutlets on paper towels. Season with salt and pepper to taste. Lightly dredge both sides of 4 cutlets in flour, patting off excess.

2   Heat 2 tablespoons olive oil in a very large nonstick skillet (or use 2) over high heat. When oil is very hot, add floured cutlets. Brown first side until light gold, then turn and cook until not quite cooked through, 2 to 3 minutes total. Transfer to a platter. Flour remaining cutlets. Add remaining 1 tablespoon oil to skillet. Cook cutlets in same fashion. Remove skillet from heat. Return first cutlets to skillet. Arrange all in one layer, overlapping if necessary. Pour lemon juice over cutlets.

3 Lay 1 slice mozzarella over each cutlet. Slide skillet under broiler to melt cheese, 1 to 2 minutes. Serve cutlets right away with pan juices spooned on top.

4 SERVINGS

other ideas

SIMPLE TIPS *The cutlets are slightly undercooked when they're sautéed so they won't overcook when the cheese is melting.*

Instead of melting the cheese under the broiler, cover the skillet tightly and let it melt over low heat on top of the stove.

You don't need to use an ovenproof skillet as long as its handle doesn't go under the heat element.

SERVING SUGGESTIONS *Baked butternut squash and spinach or Swiss chard, or Artichoke Hearts with Onion, Balsamic Vinegar, and Parmesan Cheese (page 172). Warm, crisp bread or buttered orzo sprinkled with fresh basil or oregano.*

VARIATIONS *Use chicken, pork, or veal in place of turkey.*

Scatter 2 teaspoons capers over the top of the dish when serving.

Roast Turkey Breast with Potatoes, Marjoram, and Sage

Turkey may seem all-American, but Italians have embraced it in a variety of culinary ways for years. In fact, it's a favorite on many holiday tables there, just like here. Roasting half a turkey breast does takes a little time, but it makes for plenty of servings, with maybe even enough for leftovers. Not to mention, once it's in the oven you can go about your merry way while the turkey is readying itself for dinner.

6 medium baking potatoes (about 2 pounds)
1 turkey breast half with skin and bone (about 2 $1/2$ pounds)
2 tablespoons extra-virgin olive oil
1 tablespoon chopped fresh marjoram
1 tablespoon chopped fresh sage
1 cup chicken broth

1   Preheat oven to 350°F with rack in center. Peel potatoes and cut in half lengthwise. Place turkey breast in roasting pan just large enough to hold it when potatoes are added. Rub turkey with 1 tablespoon olive oil, sprinkle with marjoram, and season with salt and pepper to taste. Toss potatoes with remaining 1 tablespoon olive oil, sage, and salt and pepper to taste in large bowl. Arrange potatoes around turkey.

2 Roast 45 minutes. Using a metal spatula, scrape up and turn potatoes in pan. Continue roasting until a meat thermometer inserted in thickest part of turkey reads 170°F, about 45 minutes. Transfer turkey and potatoes to a platter and loosely cover with foil to keep warm. Let stand 10 minutes before carving. (If potatoes aren't quite done, increase oven temperature to 400°F, return potatoes to pan, and continue roasting until tender.)

3 Pour off fat from roasting pan. Place pan over medium-high heat. Add broth and bring to a boil, scraping up browned bits with wooden or metal spatula. Boil until flavorful and reduced by half, about 5 minutes. Carve turkey breast. Moisten slices with juices and serve remaining juices on side. Serve right away.

6 SERVINGS

other ideas

SERVING SUGGESTIONS *Carrots with Olive Oil and Oregano (page 178). Or tender sautéed green cabbage with mushrooms. Or try the Green Beans with Radicchio (page 182).*

VARIATIONS *Replace the fresh marjoram for the turkey with 1/2 teaspoon dried marjoram.*

Replace the fresh sage in the potatoes with about 2 teaspoons crumbled dried leaves.

Scatter 10 to 12 unpeeled garlic cloves over the potatoes and roast together. Serve the whole cloves on the platter with the potatoes and each person can peel his own.

Sprinkle the potatoes with 1 or 2 minced garlic cloves 1 or 2 minutes before they are done, stirring them into the potatoes as best as possible.

Replace 1/4 to 1/3 cup of broth for the final pan juices with the same amount of dry white wine.

e simpler the better # Beef, Lamb, Pork, and Veal

Beef Patties with Red Wine and Provolone	122
Tuscan-Style Grilled Steak	124
Steak with Red Wine, Olives, and Peperoncini	126
Old-Fashioned Meatballs in Red Sauce	128
Pot Roast with Red Wine, Italian Style	130
Lamb Steaks with Mint Pesto	132
Lamb Stew with Garlic, Tomatoes, and Rosemary	134
Pork Chops Braised with Marsala	136
Pork Chops with White Wine Tomato Sauce	138
Sausages with Cannellini Beans and Tomatoes	140
Spareribs with White Wine, Rosemary, and Black Pepper	142
Veal Chops with Hazelnuts and Lemon Cream	144
Veal Scallopini with Lemon, Garlic, and Bay Leaf	146
Calf's Liver with Balsamic Honey Onions	148

Beef Patties with Red Wine and Provolone

Shaped like big burgers, these meat loaves are robustly seasoned with the help of shredded provolone cheese. Red wine is stirred into the ground meat, too, which brings a sophisticated touch to the taste when the patties are cooked.

$^3/_4$ cup plain dry bread crumbs

$^1/_2$ cup red wine

1 egg

2 tablespoons tomato paste

1$^3/_4$ pounds ground sirloin or round

1 loose cup shredded sharp provolone cheese

2 tablespoons extra-virgin olive oil

1 Preheat oven to 350°F. Soak $^1/_4$ cup bread crumbs in red wine in a small bowl until softened, 5 minutes. The wine won't be completely absorbed. Lightly beat egg in large bowl. Whisk in tomato paste. Whisk in softened bread crumbs. Season with $^1/_2$ teaspoon salt and a few grinds of pepper. Crumble meat into bowl. Sprinkle cheese on top. Combine ingredients well with fork.

2 Form into four 1-inch-thick patties. Place remaining $^1/_2$ cup bread crumbs on a plate. Dip both sides of patties into crumbs, pressing lightly to adhere. Heat olive oil in very

large ovenproof, nonstick skillet (or use 2) over medium heat. Add patties and brown first side, 3 minutes. Turn and lightly brown second side, 1 minute.

3 Place skillet in oven and cook, without turning, until patties are just cooked through, about 12 minutes. Serve right away.

4 SERVINGS

other ideas

SIMPLE TIPS *Let the ground meat sit at room temperature for an hour. It will be easier to combine with the seasonings.*

Dip the patties in bread crumbs right before cooking so the crumbs don't turn soggy and stick in the skillet.

An ovenproof skillet with a regular surface will work, too. Just be sure the olive oil is good and hot before putting in the patties.

SERVING SUGGESTIONS *Romaine salad with tomatoes, sautéed eggplant, or Green Beans and Zucchini with Potatoes (page 184). Garlic bread or plain Italian bread with olive oil on the side for dipping, or roasted potatoes.*

Tuscan-Style Grilled Steak

To talk about Tuscan steak, *bistecca alla fiorentina,* is to talk about tradition itself. The beef comes from renowned Chianina cattle and the steak preparation is utter simplicity. It is grilled over wood, and when brought to the table, seasoned with salt and Tuscan olive oil, or sometimes butter. In this ever-so-slightly dressed-up version, I've added a spoonful of red wine–olive oil sauce for drizzling over the lightly charred beef. It seamlessly joins with the steak juices to add just an extra lick of flavor.

Two 1-pound T-bone or rib eye steaks, each 1 to 1¼ inches thick
2 tablespoons extra-virgin olive oil
⅓ cup red wine
¼ teaspoon dried oregano

1   Remove steaks from refrigerator 30 to 60 minutes before cooking. Dry steaks with paper towels. Rub steaks with 1 tablespoon olive oil. Season with pepper.

2   Boil down wine in a small saucepan over low heat until syrupy and about 1½ table-spoons remain. Stir in remaining 1 tablespoon olive oil until blended. Season lightly with salt and stir in oregano. Set aside. Prepare a hot fire in the barbecue grill.

3   Grill first side of steaks until well browned, 2 to 4 minutes. Turn, and cook 2 to 4 minutes more for medium-rare. Transfer to a platter and let rest 5 minutes. Slice thinly across the grain, keeping shape of steak, and arrange on platter. Spoon red wine–olive oil over top and season with $^{1}/_{2}$ teaspoon coarse salt, or to taste. Serve right away.

4 SERVINGS

other ideas

SERVING SUGGESTIONS *Steamed Swiss chard or spinach, or Leeks Baked with Butter and Marjoram (page 186). Roasted potatoes or Italian-Style Potato Salad (page 164).*

VARIATION *Sprinkle the steak with fresh leaves of oregano instead of using the dried oregano in the red wine–olive oil sauce.*

Steak with Red Wine, Olives, and Peperoncini

Steaks are not eaten throughout Italy anywhere to the degree they are here. But when they are served, they're cooked in one of two ways: grilled over a hot hardwood fire or cut thin, then quickly seared in a seriously hot pan. This steak is the seared sort and it's complemented with a robust sauce that combines the steak juices with red wine, strong black olives, and a little warmth from Italian pickled peppers, peperoncini. However, if it's heat you're going for, double the peperoncini.

$3/4$ cup red wine

$1\frac{1}{2}$ tablespoons tomato paste

9 cured black Greek olives, such as Kalamata

1 peperoncini

Four 6-ounce boneless steaks, each $1/2$ to $3/4$ inch thick ($1\frac{1}{2}$ pounds total)

$1\frac{1}{2}$ tablespoons olive oil

1   Pour wine into small bowl. Whisk in tomato paste until smooth. Pit and coarsely chop olives. Cut peperoncini lengthwise in half. Seed and chop 1 half. Save other half for another use. Dry steaks with paper towels. Season with salt and pepper to taste.

2   Heat olive oil in large heavy skillet over high heat until smoke just starts. Add steaks

without crowding, in 2 batches if necessary. Deeply brown first side, 2 to 3 minutes. Turn and brown 2 to 3 minutes more. Steaks will be medium-rare to medium. Transfer to a platter. Cook second batch, if necessary.

3   Pour fat from skillet. Reduce heat to medium and stir in olives and peperoncini. Immediately add wine mixture. Cook down, stirring occasionally, adding platter juices, until lightly thickened and richly colored, 3 to 4 minutes. Pour over steaks and serve hot.

4 SERVINGS

other ideas

SIMPLE TIPS *Sirloin, New York strip, and even filet mignon are good steak choices.*

Peperoncini is sold in jars at the supermarket and sometimes, too, in the salad bar section near the olives.

A heavy cast-iron skillet holds and conducts heat beautifully, which makes it the perfect pan for pan-searing steaks. Other heavy skillets, such as ones made by Calphalon, would be excellent too.

Crowding the steaks in the pan creates steam. And the steam keeps the meat from browning well.

SERVING SUGGESTIONS *Escarole or broccoli rabe with garlic, cauliflower, or Baked Spinach with Garlic Bread Crumbs (page 192). Start with spaghetti with olive oil and garlic (if not serving Baked Spinach with Garlic Bread Crumbs), then serve steak. Or serve with olive oil roasted potatoes or crusty bread.*

Old-Fashioned Meatballs in Red Sauce

Most of us have a tough time saying no to the lure of a meatball. Well, here is a batch of meatballs ready for the test. These particular ones, a mixture of beef and sausage, are laid out in a pan, then smothered in crushed tomatoes and seasoned with grated Romano cheese. Then they're baked in a hot oven, which accomplishes two things. First, it saves the step of browning them on top of the stove. And second, the sauce is automatically seasoned with the savory meatball juices and zesty, salty Romano.

1 pound ground round (15 percent fat)

$1/2$ pound sweet Italian sausage

$1/3$ plain dry bread crumbs

2 eggs, lightly beaten

2 large garlic cloves, minced

$1/3$ cup grated pecorino Romano cheese

$1 3/4$ cups canned crushed tomatoes in heavy puree

1 Remove ground round and sausage from refrigerator 30 to 60 minutes before cooking, if possible. Place bread crumbs in large bowl and stir in $1/3$ cup water. When absorbed, blend together with eggs, garlic, $1/4$ cup grated Romano, $1/4$ teaspoon salt, and $1/4$ teaspoon pepper.

2 Preheat oven to 425°F. Add meats to bread crumb mixture and combine well with fork. Form into 12 even balls. Lay in 1 layer in 8 x 14-inch baking dish so each is separated by about 1 inch.

3 Stir $1/4$ cup water into crushed tomatoes and season with $1/8$ teaspoon salt and pepper to taste. Pour tomatoes over and around meatballs. Sprinkle tops with remaining $1 1/3$ tablespoons grated Romano. Bake in center of oven until meatballs are just cooked through, about 18 minutes. Serve hot.

MAKES TWELVE $2 1/2$-INCH MEATBALLS

other ideas

SIMPLE TIPS *The 15 percent fat in the ground round is enough to add good flavor but not so much that the sauce needs degreasing after cooking.*

Blending the bread crumbs, eggs, and other seasonings together first enables them to be mixed more thoroughly with the meats.

SERVING SUGGESTIONS *Broccoli rabe or spinach with garlic. And buttered macaroni or warm, crusty Italian bread.*

DRESS IT UP *Serve the meatballs under a blanket of mozzarella. One-half pound of fresh mozzarella makes 12 slices, just right for this purpose. About 2 minutes before the meatballs are done, lay 1 slice of cheese on top of each. Finish cooking until the cheese is melted, then bring the dish to the table and scatter with fresh basil.*

VARIATIONS *Use all ground round and leave out the sausage. Or use hot sausage in place of sweet.*

Use a prepared tomato sauce in place of the crushed tomatoes.

Pot Roast with Red Wine, Italian Style

A good pot roast always takes its own, sweet time. But it's quick to start. So if you have a few hours at home with other things to do, then get the roast going first, slip it into the oven, and leave it to do its own thing. You'll notice when you look at the ingredients that anchovies are listed: They're little pieces inserted into the beef the way you would slivers of garlic into a leg of lamb. Maybe that dismays you. But what they do is add depth of flavor along with the wine, onions, and tomatoes in the dish. You won't even notice they're there. But of course you can always leave them out.

2 medium onions

1 cup drained canned tomatoes

2 large or 3 small anchovy fillets

3 pounds boneless chuck in 1 piece, about 2 1/2 inches thick

2 tablespoons extra-virgin olive oil

1 cup red wine

1   Preheat oven to 350°F. Thinly slice onions. Coarsely chop tomatoes. Cut anchovies into 1/2-inch lengths. Dry meat with paper towels. Cut 1/2-inch slits into both sides

of meat. Insert an anchovy piece in each using a paring knife, if necessary, to poke the anchovies into the slits. Season meat with salt and pepper to taste.

2 Heat olive oil over medium-high heat in a Dutch oven or stew pot that fits meat somewhat snugly. Brown first side of meat well, 3 to 5 minutes. Turn and brown other side, 3 to 5 minutes. Stand on edges to brown, 2 minutes each edge. Remove meat. Add onions, reduce heat to medium-low, and cook, stirring occasionally, until golden, about 8 minutes. Stir in tomatoes and cook 1 minute. Add wine and reduce by about one-fourth, 2 to 3 minutes.

3 Return meat to pot, cover, and place in oven. Cook, turning once or twice, until meat is fork-tender, about $2^{1}/_{2}$ hours. Season to taste with salt and pepper. Slice thinly across the grain, spoon pan juices over top, and serve.

4 TO 6 SERVINGS

other ideas

SERVING SUGGESTIONS *Roasted radicchio, escarole with garlic, or peas. Soft polenta, mashed potatoes, or buttered noodles.*

VARIATIONS *Leave out the anchovies and crumble a beef bouillion cube into the pot instead.*

Mash the chopped anchovies into the cooked onions in the pot before adding the tomatoes.

Lamb Steaks with Mint Pesto

Most of us immediately think "basil" when pesto is mentioned. But these days, other fresh herbs increasingly take its place or are used in combination with basil. This version is made from fresh mint, and it supplies just the right fragrant accent for lamb steaks or chops, whether they're broiled or grilled. Lamb steak, the choice here, is a cross-cut section from the leg of lamb and is an especially flavorful, meaty choice.

1 large garlic clove

1 $1/2$ cups packed fresh mint leaves (from one 6-ounce bunch)

$1/4$ cup freshly grated Parmesan cheese

1 tablespoon pine nuts

$1/4$ cup extra-virgin olive oil

4 lamb steaks, 9 ounces each and about 1 inch thick

1   With machine running, drop garlic clove through feed tube of food processor fitted with metal blade. Add mint, Parmesan, and pine nuts. Process until very finely chopped. With machine running, gradually add olive oil. Season with salt and pepper to taste. Transfer to serving bowl and cover with plastic wrap, pressing wrap directly onto surface of pesto.

2 Preheat broiler with rack 4 inches from heat source. Lightly oil broiler rack. Season lamb steaks with salt and pepper to taste. Broil, turning once, until both sides are browned, about 6 minutes. They will be medium-rare.

3 Serve lamb steaks right away with a dollop of pesto on top of each.

4 SERVINGS

other ideas

SIMPLE TIPS *Pesto has a tendency to discolor when it's exposed to air. So, to help keep that from happening, press a piece of plastic wrap directly on its surface to keep the air out. However, if the pesto does discolor, don't worry; just give it a good stir before serving.*

If you have any fresh parsley in the kitchen, add a couple of tablespoons of leaves when you're making the pesto—its chlorophyll will help prevent discoloration.

To tell if the lamb is medium-rare, press the steak with your forefinger. If the steak feels slightly soft with just a bit of resilience, it is medium-rare. Cook the lamb longer, if you wish, of course.

SERVING SUGGESTIONS *Green beans, carrots, or Green Beans and Zucchini with Potatoes (page 184). If not serving the latter, serve orzo tossed with olive oil and crumbled goat cheese.*

VARIATIONS *Substitute fresh basil for half of the mint, or use all basil. You can also use chopped walnuts or blanched almonds instead of the pine nuts.*

If you wish, cook the lamb steaks on an outside barbecue grill over hot coals covered with white ash. For a gas grill, use the High setting to be sure you get a nice, brown crust on the meat. And be sure to oil the grill grate just before cooking.

Lamb Stew with Garlic, Tomatoes, and Rosemary

Unlike a traditional American stew where the meat is fully covered in a thickened broth the whole time it cooks, this Italian-style lamb stew calls for much less liquid—in this case white wine. The wine cooks down and combines with the other flavorings as the chunks of lamb slowly simmer. And when the meat has become fork-tender, it's coated in richly reduced, garlicky pan juices deeply flavored with tomato.

6 garlic cloves
$1/2$ cup drained canned tomatoes
2 pounds boneless shoulder lamb, cut into $1^1/2$- to 2-inch cubes
3 tablespoons extra-virgin olive oil
3-inch sprig fresh rosemary
$3/4$ cup dry white wine

1 Preheat oven to 350°F. Lightly crush garlic with side of knife. Coarsely chop tomatoes. Dry lamb with paper towels. Heat olive oil in a medium stew pot or large saucepan over low heat. Add garlic and rosemary and cook, turning garlic occasionally, until light gold, about 8 minutes. Remove garlic and rosemary and set aside.

2 Increase heat to medium-high under pot and brown meat in batches without crowding, about 3 minutes a batch. Remove meat as each batch is browned. Pour off excess

fat and reduce heat to low. Add wine and scrape up browned bits on bottom of pot, 1 minute. Return meat and juices to pot along with garlic and rosemary. Add tomatoes and bring to a simmer.

3 Cover pot and bake until meat is very tender and only a small amount of rich pan juices remain, $1^{1}/_{2}$ hours, adding more tablespoons of wine or water at any point if the juices reduce too much. Discard rosemary stem and season to taste with salt and pepper. Serve hot.

4 SERVINGS

other ideas

SIMPLE TIP *The sides of the pot will have good-tasting cooking juices stuck to them as the stew cooks. Bring up some of the pot juices with a spoon to loosen and scrape them back into the rest.*

SERVING SUGGESTIONS *Broccoli rabe or cauliflower. Or a bitter greens salad sprinkled with goat cheese. Pasta tossed with cream and a little grated cheese or Baked Potatoes with Romano Cheese (page 198).*

VARIATIONS *Use $^{3}/_{4}$ teaspoon dried rosemary in place of the fresh, adding it with the tomatoes.*

Boneless lamb shoulder isn't always easy to get. Many supermarkets carry lamb neck, with the bones, as their lamb stew meat. To use lamb neck, buy about $^{1}/_{2}$ pound extra to compensate for the added weight of the bones.

Pork Chops Braised with Marsala

Pork chops cooked the Italian way take longer in the pan. But once they're going, all it takes is an occasional peek to check on their progress. The chops are cooked beyond when their meat is tinged with pink or just cooked through, their first stage of tenderness. And then they toughen. But when the chops reach the last stage they turn tender once again. And their Marsala and tomato flavorings have become a small amount of concentrated sauce accented with the anise taste of fennel seeds. These chops are inspired by Marcella Hazan's wonderful Pork Chops Braised with Marsala and Red Wine.

1 garlic clove

4 pork chops, 8 ounces each and $1/2$ inch thick

$1 1/2$ tablespoons extra-virgin olive oil

$1/4$ cup crushed tomatoes in heavy puree

$1/2$ cup dry Marsala

$1/4$ teaspoon fennel seeds

1 Chop garlic. Dry pork chops with paper towels. Season with salt and pepper to taste. Heat olive oil over medium heat in skillet large enough to snugly hold chops in 1 layer. When hot, lightly brown chops on both sides, 5 to 6 minutes total. Remove

chops. Reduce heat to lowest possible and stir in garlic. Immediately add tomatoes, Marsala, and fennel seeds. Return chops to skillet and cover.

2   Cook 20 minutes. Turn chops, cover, and cook 20 minutes more. Check liquid in skillet. If thick and starting to stick, stir in 3 to 4 tablespoons water. Turn chops again, cover, and cook 10 to 15 minutes more, checking sauce occasionally and adding a little water, if necessary.

3   Chops are done if tender when pierced with sharp fork or skewer. Sauce should be thick and concentrated. Season with salt and pepper to taste. Turn chops into sauce to coat and serve hot.

4 SERVINGS

other ideas

SIMPLE TIPS *A skillet that leaves space around the chops will allow the Marsala and tomato to cook down more rapidly. So keep a close eye on the liquid as the chops cook. More frequent additions of water will probably be needed. Make them small additions, though, to keep the dish its most flavorful.*

If the sauce is too thin when the chops are done, remove them and cook down the sauce for a minute or two. Add the chops back to the skillet and turn them in the sauce to coat.

SERVING SUGGESTIONS *Sautéed kale, cabbage, or broccoli rabe, or lentils with garlic. Buttered rice tossed with shredded mozzarella cheese or cannellini beans, or sliced potatoes baked with olive oil.*

Pork Chops with White Wine Tomato Sauce

It's easy to think of tomato sauce as just this basic, good thing. And it is, but it also readily takes on all sorts of styles: garlicky and spicy, rich with savory cured meat, or fragrant with herbs, to mention just a few. And its character changes, too, depending on whether it's made with fresh or canned tomatoes. This tomato sauce is scented with lemon peel and lightened by white wine, and the whole dish couldn't be easier to make. First, brown the pork, add the sauce ingredients, then simmer together until the meat is done and the tomatoes have thickened to become a flavorful spoonful for the top of each chop.

4 boneless pork chops, 7 ounces each and $3/4$ to 1 inch thick
$1^{1}/_{2}$ teaspoons extra-virgin olive oil
2 strips lemon peel, each about 1 x 2 inches
$^{1}/_{2}$ cup white wine
$^{1}/_{2}$ cup crushed tomatoes in heavy puree

1   Dry pork chops on paper towels. Season with salt and pepper to taste.

2   Heat olive oil in large skillet over medium-high heat. Add chops and brown first side until golden, 3 to 4 minutes. Stand on fat edge to crisp, 1 minute. Add lemon peel,

then lay chops on second side to lightly brown, 1 to 2 minutes. Reduce heat to low and add wine and tomatoes. Cover and simmer until chops are just cooked through, about 5 minutes.

3   Transfer chops to plates. Discard lemon peel and boil down sauce over medium heat until thickened, stirring occasionally, 2 to 3 minutes. Season with salt and pepper to taste. Top each chop with a spoonful of sauce and serve hot.

4 SERVINGS

other ideas

SIMPLE TIP *The white pith right under the yellow lemon skin is bitter. Be sure to trim it off with a paring knife before you add the strips to the pan.*

SERVING SUGGESTIONS *Zucchini sautéed until tender or spinach with garlic. Pasta tossed with butter and grated cheese or Fresh Linguine with Butter, Parmesan Cheese, and Mushrooms (page 46).*

VARIATION *Veal chops and boneless chicken breasts are good prepared this way, too. So are fish fillets such as salmon and thick swordfish and tuna steaks.*

Sausages with Cannellini Beans and Tomatoes

When I want something to eat that is simple, soul-satisfying, and homey, I often think of these sausages in their sage-scented tomato sauce with creamy white beans. Particularly if I'm thinking about dinner on a blustery winter's day and eager to serve something hearty to warm the bones.

1 medium to large onion

3 large garlic cloves

15 fresh sage leaves

$1^3/_4$ pounds Italian pork sausage links

One 28-ounce can Italian plum tomatoes in juice

One 15-ounce can cannellini beans

$^1/_4$ cup extra-virgin olive oil

1 Chop onion and garlic. Chop sage. Prick each sausage with a sharp fork several times. Save juices and coarsely chop tomatoes. Drain and rinse beans.

2 Heat olive oil in a large, deep skillet or Dutch oven over medium heat. Brown sausages on all sides, about 3 minutes, then remove. Reduce heat to low and stir in onion. Cook until golden brown, stirring occasionally, about 10 minutes. Stir in garlic and sage and cook 1 minute, stirring. Return sausages to pot.

3 Add tomatoes with their juices and beans. Bring to a simmer, partially cover, and cook, turning sausages once or twice, about 15 minutes or until cooked through. Season to taste with salt and pepper and serve hot.

4 SERVINGS

other ideas

SERVING SUGGESTIONS *Sautéed eggplant with parsley or steamed Swiss chard. Orzo with butter and grated Parmesan or Romano cheese.*

VARIATIONS *Use hot sausage links in place of the sweet, or a mixture.*

Substitute 1 3/4 teaspoons rubbed dried sage or 1 teaspoon dried marjoram for the fresh sage.

Spareribs with White Wine, Rosemary, and Black Pepper

We don't hear much about Italian spareribs. But they are part of the cuisine and delicious. Here, the ribs cook in wine in a covered pan with rosemary, which marries its pinelike flavor with the sweet meat. And when the ribs are done, the pan juices have turned into a rich, thick sauce, just enough to coat them. The black pepper, stirred in at the end, adds taste to the dish without the heat its name can imply.

3 1/2 pounds meaty pork spareribs
1 tablespoon fresh rosemary leaves
2 tablespoons extra-virgin olive oil
4 garlic cloves
1 1/4 cups white wine

1 Trim fat from spareribs, then cut between bones into individual ribs. Finely chop fresh rosemary. Dry ribs with paper towels, then season lightly with pepper and salt to taste. Warm olive oil over low heat in a large, deep skillet or Dutch oven that fits ribs in no more than 1 1/2 layers. Add garlic and cook, turning occasionally, until golden, 5 to 7 minutes. Remove and set aside.

2 Increase heat to medium-high. In batches, brown both sides of ribs, removing each

when done, 8 to 10 minutes total. Pour off fat. Return ribs to pot and reduce heat to as low as possible. Sprinkle with rosemary. Return garlic. Pour wine over all and scrape brown residue on bottom of pan into wine. Cook 30 seconds and cover.

3 Cook 20 minutes, then turn ribs. Cover and cook 10 to 15 minutes more. The juices should be thickened and beginning to stick to pan bottom. Stir in $1/4$ to $1/2$ cup water depending on thickness, cover, and cook until ribs are tender, 10 to 15 minutes more. Check occasionally to see if sauce is sticking. If so, add a little more water. When done, sauce should be thick enough to heavily coat ribs. Stir in $1/2$ teaspoon freshly ground pepper and turn ribs into sauce to coat. Serve hot.

4 SERVINGS

other ideas

SIMPLE TIPS *Some or all of the ribs can cook on their sides so more can fit comfortably in the pan.*

Pierce the meaty part of a rib with a sharp fork or skewer to see if it's done.

If the sauce isn't thick enough by the end, remove the ribs and cook it down, stirring. Stir in the pepper, then return the ribs and roll them in the sauce to coat and rewarm.

SERVING SUGGESTIONS *Baked or grilled fennel, broiled tomato halves, or Tossed Cauliflower Salad (page 158). Short pasta tossed with butter and a little grated cheese or baked potatoes or boiled new potatoes drizzled with olive oil.*

VARIATION *Replace the fresh rosemary with 1 teaspoon dried.*

Veal Chops with Hazelnuts and Lemon Cream

Luxurious in all ways, these luscious veal chops are sautéed over low heat and turned frequently as they cook, which keeps the delicate meat tender, cooks them evenly, and slowly turns them golden brown. At the end, a big splash of cream releases the brown bits that have stuck to the pan during cooking and makes them part of the rich, lemony sauce.

2 lemons

3/4 cup heavy cream

1/4 cup skinned hazelnuts

4 veal chops, 10 to 12 ounces each and 3/4 to 1 inch thick

2 tablespoons butter

1   Grate lemon zest. Mix with cream in small bowl. Coarsely chop hazelnuts. Dry veal chops on paper towels. Season with salt and pepper to taste.

2   Melt butter in large skillet over medium heat until it froths. Lightly brown first side of chops, 3 minutes. Turn, then reduce heat to low. Cook chops, turning 3 or 4 times, until golden brown on both sides and slightly pink in center, 15 to 18 minutes. Cook a few minutes longer for well done. Transfer chops to platter.

3 Add hazelnuts to butter remaining in skillet. Toast, stirring frequently, until spotted light brown, 2 to 3 minutes. Add lemon cream and scrape up browned bits from pan bottom, stirring frequently. Cook until lightly thickened, 1 to 2 minutes. Return chops and platter juices to skillet. Turn chops in sauce to coat. Warm 30 to 60 seconds. Serve chops with sauce on top. Grind a little pepper over each and serve right away.

4 SERVINGS

other ideas

SIMPLE TIPS *In addition to turning the chops frequently, moving them around in the pan once in a while helps keep the butter from turning no darker than light brown. Nut brown butter is delicious but it can burn quickly after that.*

The sauce has thickened enough when it lightly coats a spoon.

SERVING SUGGESTIONS *Green beans, broccoli, or Baked Spinach with Garlic Bread Crumbs (page 192). Rice pilaf or lightly buttered angel hair pasta.*

VARIATION *Pork chops are a good replacement for the veal chops, or boneless chicken breasts. And walnuts can substitute for the hazelnuts.*

Veal Scallopini with Lemon, Garlic, and Bay

Good quality veal is pale pink in color, sweetly mild in flavor, and pricey. Doing it justice, I think, requires seasonings that both highlight its delicacy and offer a bit of a lift. In this simple dish, first garlic cloves and bay leaves are gently cooked in oil until the garlic turns gold and the bay slightly browned, each offering a subtle scent to the oil. Then the thin slices of veal are rapidly sautéed, just long enough to brown the outsides and keep the juices inside. When lemon juice and butter are added to the pan to scrape up the stuck-on little bits of flavor, that's the only extra bit of savoriness the meat needs.

5 tablespoons vegetable oil

6 large garlic cloves, lightly crushed

4 large bay leaves

1½ pounds veal scallopini

Flour

2½ tablespoons freshly squeezed lemon juice

2 tablespoons butter

1   Heat oil in very large skillet over low heat with garlic and bay leaves. Cook, turning

garlic occasionally, until golden, 8 to 10 minutes. Discard garlic and push bay leaves to edge of pan.

2 Dry veal on paper towels. Season with salt and pepper to taste. Flour both sides and pat off excess. Increase heat under skillet to high, then discard bay leaves as they brown. Doing half the veal at a time, brown first side, 1 to 2 minutes. Turn and cook second side, 1 to 2 minutes. Transfer to platter. Sauté remaining veal and transfer to platter when done.

3 Remove skillet from heat. Add lemon juice and butter. Scrape up browned bits from pan bottom as butter melts, 15 to 30 seconds. Pour pan juices over scallopini and serve right away.

4 SERVINGS

other ideas

SIMPLE TIPS *Press lightly on the garlic cloves and bay leaves as they cook to release a bit more of their flavor.*

Flour the scallopini just before sautéing so they don't become soggy.

Hold the cooked scallopini in a single layer on a warm platter as the rest are being cooked. They won't cool down as quickly or turn soggy from being stacked or overlapped.

SERVING SUGGESTIONS *Sautéed Swiss chard or the Mesclun Salad with Ricotta and Pine Nuts (page 160) served after the veal. Polenta or ciabatta bread with a cucumber, red onion, and tomato salad.*

VARIATION *Turkey, chicken, and pork scallopini work well, too.*

Calf's Liver with Balsamic Honey Onions

The Venetians are famous for their sweet-and-sour dishes, and their rendition of calf's liver smothered in meltingly tender onions is probably the best known. Italian cooks don't have the super-sweet onions we have in the States, like the Walla Walla or Maui. But what they do have is the style to take this most humble of vegetable, the yellow onion, and cook it long and slowly to develop its deep, natural sweetness. And here they're enhanced with sweet vinegar and sweet honey. The onions themselves take about 30 minutes to prepare, but once they're done, the liver cooks very quickly.

2 tablespoons butter

2 large yellow onions, thinly sliced

2 tablespoons balsamic vinegar

1 tablespoon honey

3 tablespoons extra-virgin olive oil

1 1/4 pounds calf's liver, cut into six 1/2-inch-thick slices

1/3 cup all-purpose flour

1 Melt butter in large skillet over medium-high heat. Add onions and cook, stirring occasionally, until wilted, about 5 minutes. Cover and reduce heat to low. Cook, stirring occasionally, until soft and nicely browned, about 20 minutes. Stir in vinegar and

honey. Cook, uncovered, stirring often, until onions are very tender and liquid reduced to a glaze, about 10 minutes. Season with salt and pepper to taste. Heap in the center of a platter and cover with foil to keep warm. Wash and dry skillet.

2   Add olive oil to skillet over medium-high heat until very hot but not smoking. Dry liver on paper towels. Make a few shallow cuts around outside of each liver slice to prevent curling. Season with salt and pepper to taste. Dip in flour, pat off excess, and add slices to skillet without crowding. Cook until underside is browned and crisp, 2 to 3 minutes. Turn and brown other side, 2 to 3 minutes more. Liver will be slightly pink in center.

3   Overlap liver slices over onions and serve right away.

4 TO 6 SERVINGS

other ideas

SIMPLE TIPS *A whole calf's liver is surrounded by a thin membrane that should be peeled off by the butcher before he cuts the liver into slices. Unfortunately, that step is sometimes ignored and you can see this shiny, tough little membrane running around the edge of each slice. If that's the case, merely peel it off from one end with a paring knife.*

Liver creates a lot of pan juices, which can make for a messy skillet. Simply add a couple of cups of water to the skillet and bring to a boil over high heat. Let stand for a few minutes, and the juices will loosen to make cleaning a lot easier.

SERVING SUGGESTIONS *Sautéed spinach or Baked Spinach with Garlic Bread Crumbs (page 192). Roasted or boiled red-skinned potatoes, tossed with olive oil.*

VARIATION *If you're a liver fan, try sautéed chicken livers with these onions, too. Or sautéed pork chops*

the simpler the better Salads

Arugula and Basil Salad 152

Arugula, Blood Orange, and Fennel Salad 154

Shredded Beet and Gorgonzola Salad 156

Tossed Cauliflower Salad 158

Mesclun Salad with Ricotta and Pine Nuts 160

Summer Sweet Pepper, Tomato, and Onion Salad with Basil 162

Italian-Style Potato Salad 164

Rice Salad with Green Dressing 166

Seafood Salad with Mint and Scallion 168

Arugula and Basil Salad

Olive oil and lemon juice make the lightest and most versatile of dressings, whether mixed with vegetables, drizzled over seafood of any sort, or as the finish for green, leafy salads. Arugula, with its tantalizing hint of all things Italian, is one perfect recipient. Then when you toss in a big handful of fresh basil, the salad becomes a pleasure in differences: slightly spicy leaves and sweet herbs all glossed in slightly sharp citrus dressing.

1 large or 2 smaller bunches arugula
1 loosely packed cup fresh basil leaves
2 tablespoons extra-virgin olive oil
1 teaspoon freshly squeezed lemon juice

1   Trim any coarse stems from arugula, then wash and dry enough to measure 8 loosely packed cups. Wash and dry basil leaves. Place all in large salad bowl.

2   Toss with olive oil to lightly coat leaves. Then toss with lemon juice and season with salt to taste.

3 Divide among plates. Grind a little pepper over each and serve right away.

4 SERVINGS

SIMPLE TIPS *Choose the smaller leaves from the bunch of basil. If they're all large, then tear them into smaller pieces.*

Toss any green salad with olive oil first. It keeps the lemon juice or vinegar from wilting the leaves.

VARIATION *Use half watercress and half arugula. Or use only watercress.*

Arugula, Blood Orange, and Fennel Salad

Arugula is a lightly peppery-tasting leaf, and for some of us a salad of it is almost an addiction. Delicious by itself dressed merely with vinegar or lemon juice and olive oil, it's also irresistible paired with thin slices of blood orange and slivered raw fennel. Available during a short winter season, blood oranges are blushed a beautiful garnet color with a rich taste subtly suggesting spice. All together, the salad is refreshingly light and light on vinegar as the orange supplies more gentle acid in each bite.

1 to 2 bunches arugula

1 small fennel bulb

2 blood oranges or 1 large navel orange

2 tablespoons extra-virgin olive oil

2 teaspoons balsamic vinegar

1 Trim any coarse stems from the arugula, then wash and dry enough to measure 8 loosely packed cups. Place in large salad bowl. Cut fennel in half from top to bottom, then cut out core and discard. Peel off fennel layers and finely sliver enough to measure $2/3$ cup. Peel oranges and cut 16 thin slices.

2 Scatter fennel over arugula. Toss with olive oil. Then toss with vinegar and season with salt.

3 Divide among plates. Lay 4 slightly overlapping slices of orange over each salad. Grind a little pepper over top and serve right away.

4 SERVINGS

other ideas

SIMPLE TIPS *The outer layer of fennel is coarse and fibrous. Save it for cooking, if you like, or discard it. Use the more tender layers for eating raw.*

To slice an orange completely clean of membrane, don't peel it first. Cut a thin slice off the top and bottom, then stand it on a flat end. Position the blade of a large knife at the top just behind the rind next to the flesh. Cut down with a slight sawing motion to remove that section of rind. Then continue cutting around the orange in the same fashion until it's completely trimmed. Now slice it.

VARIATIONS *Scatter a small amount of very thinly sliced red onion over the top.*

In southern Italy, they serve the oranges alone, very thinly sliced and drizzled with good olive oil and seasoned with salt and pepper. It's delicious.

Shredded Beet and Gorgonzola Salad

Beets are in the love 'em or leave 'em category. Personally, I love 'em. However, if you or anyone in your family is on the fence, then it's good to know that new preparation methods have gained converts for this humble root vegetable. If you have a food processor or other mechanical shredder, you can skip cooking the beets altogether and create a gorgeous salad from raw beets. Tossed with sharp, tangy Gorgonzola with olive oil and vinegar, the dressing becomes an exciting foil for the earthy-sweet beets. Normally I recommend authentic Gorgonzola from Italy, but its soft, creamy consistency makes it difficult to crumble. So the domestic version, which is drier and often sold already crumbled, works well here.

3 large beets, greens trimmed (1 $1/4$ pounds trimmed weight)
1 $1/2$ tablespoons red wine vinegar
$1/3$ cup extra-virgin olive oil
$1/2$ cup (2 ounces) crumbled Gorgonzola cheese
2 tablespoons chopped parsley

1 Rinse the beets under cold running water, making sure to remove any traces of soil. Dry on paper towels. Peel the beets with a sturdy vegetable peeler to remove all skin.

2 Shred the beets in a food processor fitted with the large-hole metal shredding blade.

3 Place vinegar in large bowl and whisk in olive oil. Add the beets and toss to coat well. Add the cheese and parsley and toss gently to combine. Season with salt and pepper to taste. Serve right away.

4 SERVINGS

other ideas

SIMPLE TIPS *Vegetable peelers that are ergonomically designed for your hand, such as the Oxo brand, are the best and by far the easiest to use.*

To keep beet juice from staining your hands, wear rubber gloves or rub your hands lightly with vegetable oil first. After peeling, moisten your hands with water, rub with coarse salt, and then wash.

DRESS IT UP *Using 1/3 cup toasted, skinned, and coarsely chopped hazelnuts makes a perfect crunchy addition to the salad, whether it be beets alone or with the butter lettuce below.*

Dress up an already lovely green salad with the beet salad. Start by making a double batch of dressing, then pour half into a salad bowl for the greens. Make the beet salad in the first bowl. Wash and dry 1 head butter or Boston lettuce, tear into pieces, and add to the salad bowl. Toss with the dressing and season with salt and pepper. Divide the lettuce onto salad plates, and top with the beets.

VARIATION *If you love authentic Gorgonzola cheese and don't want to substitute, then whisk the "real McCoy" into the dressing before tossing it with the beets. The beets won't have the same pristine, pretty appearance but they sure will have lots of taste.*

Tossed Cauliflower Salad

Cooked in lightly boiling water, then tossed with vinegar, olive oil, and just a touch of cream, cauliflower shows off its delicate sweet side. Preparing it in this fashion allows the oftentimes pungent vegetable to let go of its cooked cabbage personality. Even for noncauliflower eaters, this little dish of snow-white florets may come as a refreshing surprise. Serve it with the meal or as part of a before-dinner antipasto.

1 small head cauliflower
1 tablespoon white wine vinegar
3 tablespoons heavy cream
1 1/2 tablespoons extra-virgin olive oil
Pinch crushed red pepper flakes
1 tablespoon chopped fresh basil

1   Bring a large saucepan of salted boiling water to a boil over high heat. Trim core from cauliflower. Cut enough into 1- to 1 1/2-inch florets to measure 6 cups.

2   Cook cauliflower at a medium boil until nicely tender but not falling apart, 3 to 4 minutes. Drain well. Place in large bowl and while still warm, toss gently first with vinegar, then cream, using a rubber spatula. Toss with olive oil. Season with salt and pepper and red pepper flakes to taste.

3 Serve warm or at room temperature sprinkled with basil.

4 TO 6 SERVINGS

other ideas

SIMPLE TIPS *Trim the stems to $^1/_2$ to 1 inch in length; the florets look most attractive that way.*

Cooking the cauliflower in a large pot of water helps remove its stronger taste and aroma.

VARIATION *Replace the basil with fresh or dried mint or oregano.*

Mesclun Salad with Ricotta and Pine Nuts

One usually expects a green salad to have some element with a kick. But this salad makes a lovely and gentle harmony of tastes: creamy bites of ricotta, buttery pine nuts, and a dressing of good olive oil with just drops of vinegar. The textures and personalities of the different lettuces, though, supply a touch of authority when it all comes together.

2 tablespoons pine nuts

2 teaspoons red wine vinegar

2 tablespoons extra-virgin olive oil

$1/2$ pound mesclun

6 tablespoons fresh ricotta cheese

1 Place pine nuts in small skillet over low heat. Toast, rolling pan frequently, until kernels have golden spots, about 3 minutes. Let cool.

2 Whisk vinegar and oil together in small bowl. Season with salt and pepper to taste.

3   Toss mesclun with pine nuts and dressing until leaves are lightly coated. Divide among plates and scatter ricotta over top in pieces. Grind fresh pepper over each and serve.

4 SERVINGS

other ideas

SIMPLE TIP *There are about 8 loosely packed cups of mesclun mixture in $1/2$ pound.*

DRESS IT UP *Ring the plate with slices of ripe avocado and slide a thin tomato wedge or two between the slices. Dress and place the salad in the center so the garnishes can be seen.*

VARIATION *For a more assertive dressing, increase the vinegar to $2 1/2$ teaspoons or to your taste. For an overall tangier result, replace the ricotta with crumbled goat cheese.*

Summer Sweet Pepper, Tomato, and Onion Salad with Basil

This crunchy salad is always a hit. First, its bright mix of colors attracts the eye as soon as it is set down on the table. Then its familiar tastes and textures make you feel right at home. Serve it as a simple salad or as part of a light meal; it's lovely with the Tossed Cauliflower Salad (page 158), along with grilled shrimp or slices of cured meat such as salami or prosciutto and, of course, hunks of good bread for sopping up the salad juices.

1 large green bell pepper

1 small red onion

2 ripe medium tomatoes

1 tablespoon extra-virgin olive oil

2 $\frac{1}{2}$ teaspoons red wine vinegar

$\frac{1}{3}$ packed cup fresh basil leaves

1 Finely dice enough bell pepper to measure $\frac{2}{3}$ cup. Cut red onion in half, then thinly slice enough to measure $\frac{1}{4}$ cup. Core, then dice tomatoes.

2   Place pepper, onion, and tomatoes into medium bowl. Drizzle first with olive oil and gently toss with rubber spatula. Drizzle with vinegar and toss again.

3   Season with salt and pepper to taste. Tear basil into bite-size pieces and fold in. Serve at room temperature.

4 SERVINGS

other ideas

DRESS IT UP *Use 1 red tomato and 1 yellow tomato. And use $1/2$ green bell pepper and $1/2$ red bell pepper, if you like, or even part of an orange bell pepper.*

VARIATION *Use grape or cherry tomatoes instead of larger tomatoes and cut them in half before tossing with the rest of the ingredients.*

Italian-Style Potato Salad

Potato salad in Italy is a whole other thing. There, it's simply the quality of the potatoes, their careful cooking, and the good vinegar and olive oil dressing that matters. Young, waxy potatoes are the ones to use because they retain their pleasingly dense, creamy texture when cooked to the just-done stage. And they can also be sliced into lovely rounds, making the salad downright elegant. Having said all this, now I can admit that I added a few goodies to jazz up this version.

1 pound small red new potatoes
1 1/2 tablespoons finely chopped onion
1 1/2 teaspoons capers
One 1/4-inch-thick slice Italian salami
2 1/2 tablespoons white wine vinegar
2 tablespoons extra-virgin olive oil

1 Bring potatoes to a boil in a large saucepan of salted water. Cook at a low boil over medium-low heat until just tender, 15 minutes. Do not overcook. Drain and let cool long enough to handle.

2   Place onion in a small strainer and rinse under cold running water. Dry on paper towels. Lightly chop capers. Cut salami into small dice. Peel potatoes and slice into $1/3$-inch-thick rounds. Lay slightly overlapping in a large shallow bowl. Scatter onion and capers over top.

3   Drizzle with vinegar and gently toss with rubber spatula. Drizzle with olive oil and toss again. Season with salt and pepper to taste and toss. Serve at room temperature with salami scattered over top.

4 SERVINGS

other ideas

SIMPLE TIP *A wooden skewer is the best way to judge if the potatoes are done. The skewer should penetrate with only the slightest resistance as it passes through the potato.*

DRESS IT UP *Cut a large ripe tomato into thin slices, then cut each slice in half. Season them with salt and place them around the salad so the cut sides lie next to the potatoes. Fresh oregano scattered over the top is a nice addition, too.*

Rice Salad with Green Dressing

This rice salad, made with short-grain Italian rice, has clear Mediterranean flavor. And that comes from seasoning the cooked rice with lots of parsley, lemon juice, capers, and fruity olive oil. Serve it as a side dish, on a buffet anytime, or in the summer as a first course or part of a picnic.

$2/3$ loosely packed cup flat-leaf parsley leaves

2 teaspoons capers

$1/4$ cup mayonnaise

$1 1/2$ tablespoons freshly squeezed lemon juice

$3/4$ cup Italian arborio rice

2 tablespoons extra-virgin olive oil

1 Mound parsley leaves and capers together. Chop finely. Place mayonnaise in large bowl. Whisk in lemon juice until smooth. Stir in parsley and capers.

2 Bring large saucepan of salted water to a boil over medium-high heat. Stir in rice. Cook at a medium boil, stirring occasionally, until grains are just tender, 10 to 12 minutes. Drain in colander and shake to remove excess water.

3 Add rice to sauce and toss with 2 forks until well combined. Season with more salt,

if you like. Divide among plates and drizzle each with its share of olive oil. Grind a little pepper over top and serve.

4 SERVINGS AS A FIRST COURSE

other ideas

SIMPLE TIPS *If the salad seems too starchy, add more mayonnaise mixed with more lemon juice.*

Do not chill this salad, as cold rice turns hard and unappetizing.

DRESS IT UP *Serve the salad as a light supper. Make a bed of crisp Romaine leaves tossed with olive oil and vinegar on a platter. Make an attractive mound of the salad on the leaves and garnish the top with crab meat, shrimp, or cooked fish broken into pieces. Surround it with quartered hard-cooked eggs, chickpeas tossed in olive oil, and strips of roasted red peppers. Or serve the salad on individual plates and lay a just-grilled fish fillet over the top of each.*

Roll teaspoonfuls of the cooled salad in small lettuce or radicchio leaves or pieces of prosciutto and serve them as part of an antipasto.

VARIATIONS *Use long-grain rice instead of arborio. It will take a few minutes longer to cook and will make a looser salad because the grains contain less starch.*

Stir some finely chopped scallion, red onion, or roasted peppers into the sauce before mixing it with the rice.

Seafood Salad with Mint and Scallion

The shrimp, scallops, and calamari that make up this salad are cooked in a skillet with olive oil for just 3 or 4 minutes. They stay succulent that way and retain all their flavor. And when tossed with mint and raw crunchy scallion, they make a light refreshing salad. Versatile, too. It's just as good slightly warm, at room temperature, or chilled. And as a main course, first course, or antipasto.

$1/2$ pound large sea scallops

$1/4$ pound calamari

$1/2$ pound small shrimp, peeled and deveined

1 medium scallion

3 tablespoons extra-virgin olive oil

1 to $1/2$ tablespoons freshly squeezed lemon juice

$3/4$ teaspoon dried mint

1   Remove small side muscle from scallops, if there, and discard. Rinse and dry with paper towels. Cut into quarters. Cut calamari into $1/3$-inch-thick rings and tentacles in half, if large. Dry shrimp on paper towels. Cut scallion into thin rounds.

2   Heat 2 tablespoons olive oil in a large nonstick skillet over medium heat. Stir in scallops, then shrimp. Cook, stirring frequently, until slightly more than half cooked,

about 2 minutes. Add calamari and cook, stirring frequently, until white, 1 to 2 minutes. The shrimp should be firm and scallops slightly springy when pressed. Transfer with slotted spoon to colander set in larger bowl. Let drain 5 minutes. Add accumulated bowl juices to juices in skillet, if saving (see Simple Tips).

3 Transfer seafood to bowl. Toss with remaining 1 tablespoon olive oil, then 1 tablespoon lemon juice or more to taste. Toss with mint and season with salt and pepper to taste. Toss with scallion if serving right away. If serving at room temperature or chilled, add just before serving.

2 MAIN-COURSE OR 4 FIRST-COURSE SERVINGS

other ideas

SIMPLE TIPS *The seafood will cook most evenly if they're in a single layer in the skillet.*

Refrigerate or freeze the pan juices. They're terrific for enriching a seafood soup or pasta.

DRESS IT UP *Serve the salad on a bed of arugula, or arugula mixed with radicchio, lightly tossed with vinegar and olive oil. Set grape or cherry tomatoes all around.*

VARIATIONS *Use bay scallops instead of sea scallops. The bay scallops will cook a minute or two faster than the shrimp, so start the shrimp first.*

Replace the squid with the meat from 10 or 12 steamed mussels. Place the mussels in the skillet with several tablespoons of water, cover, and cook 3 to 5 minutes until the shells open. Let them cool, then remove the meat. Set aside their juices if saving the shrimp and scallop juices. Add the olive oil to the skillet and cook the scallops and shrimp as in the recipe until done.

the simpler the better Side Dishes

Artichoke Hearts with Onion, Balsamic Vinegar, and Parmesan Cheese   172

Sautéed Asparagus with Onion and Mint   174

Broccoli with Black Olives and Red Wine   176

Carrots with Olive Oil and Oregano   178

Eggplant with Red Onion and Tomato   180

Green Beans with Radicchio   182

Green Beans and Zucchini with Potatoes   184

Leeks Baked with Butter and Marjoram   186

Sautéed Mushrooms with Garlic, Olive Oil, and Parsley   188

Spinach with Mascarpone   190

Baked Spinach with Garlic Bread Crumbs   192

Grilled Summer Squash with Parsley and Oregano   194

Little New Potatoes with Lemon Zest   196

Baked Potatoes with Romano Cheese   198

Arborio Rice Pilaf with Porcini Mushrooms   200

Artichoke Hearts with Onion, Balsamic Vinegar, and Parmesan Cheese

Frozen artichoke hearts are a reward for those of us who love big globe artichokes but don't always have the time to trim and cook fresh ones. Fresh or frozen, I like artichokes best when they taste clearly of themselves. All they need are simple seasonings to flatter their distinctive taste. With that in mind, these are enriched with browned onion bits, a restrained splash of balsamic vinegar, and a sprinkling of nutty grated Parmesan. The result is enhanced flavor without any of the enhancers getting the upper hand.

One 9-ounce box frozen artichoke hearts

1 small onion

3 tablespoons extra-virgin olive oil

1/2 teaspoon dried oregano

2 teaspoons balsamic vinegar

1 tablespoon grated Parmesan cheese

1   Bring medium saucepan of salted water to a boil over high heat. Add artichokes and cook until firm-tender, 4 to 5 minutes. Drain well. Finely chop onion.

2 Heat olive oil in medium skillet over medium heat. Stir in artichokes followed by onion. Sprinkle with oregano. Cook artichokes until lightly browned and onion nicely browned, stirring frequently as onion browns, 5 to 7 minutes. Reduce heat at any point if onion starts to brown too quickly.

3 Reduce heat to low and add balsamic vinegar and 1 tablespoon water. Scrape up browned bottom of pan as liquid evaporates, stirring, 1 to 2 minutes. Season to taste with salt and pepper. Serve hot, sprinkled with Parmesan cheese.

3 SERVINGS

other ideas

SIMPLE TIP *Twelve-ounce bags of frozen artichoke hearts are available in some markets. They make enough for 4, so increase the rest of the ingredients by about one-third. And if you find larger bags in a discount club, it's good to know that one 9-ounce box measures a somewhat generous 2 cups.*

DRESS IT UP *Omit the grated Parmesan and with a vegetable peeler shave strips of Parmesan from a wedge directly over the top of the artichokes.*

VARIATION *Serve the artichokes warm or at room temperature as an antipasto. Dress them with a little extra olive oil and season a little more highly with oregano and vinegar.*

Sautéed Asparagus with Onion and Mint

Asparagus and onions can act as lovely foils for one another, particularly when they're cooked together with olive oil until tender and browned. Then a finishing sprinkle of mint lifts their delicately earthy quality with its bright note. Serve the asparagus hot or warm as a side dish. Or, let it come to room temperature and present it as part of an antipasto. For me, I like the dish best after it has sat for an hour or more when the flavors have really come together.

1¼ pounds medium asparagus
1 small onion
2 tablespoons extra-virgin olive oil
1 teaspoon dried mint

1 Snap off the woody ends of the asparagus. Cut any very large spears lengthwise first, if necessary. Cut spears into 1-inch-long diagonal pieces. Very thinly slice onion.

2 Heat olive oil in a medium skillet over medium-low heat. Add asparagus and onion. Cook until vegetables are browned and tender but asparagus still firm, about 10 minutes, stirring occasionally. Reduce heat if vegetables begin to brown too much.

3   Stir in mint. Add 1 tablespoon water to release brown residue on bottom of pan to add its flavor. Let evaporate. Season vegetables with salt and pepper to taste.

4 SERVINGS

other ideas

DRESS IT UP *Scatter cooked little pieces of pancetta over the asparagus when serving.*

Or chop white button mushrooms or creminis and sauté them separately. Then combine them with the asparagus before serving, or scatter them over the top.

Broccoli with Black Olives and Red Wine

Broccoli changes dramatically in taste and appearance when cooked gently in olive oil with ripe olives, sweet tomatoes, and wine. It loses its pretty, bright green looks but gains doubly in flavor. And it can be served at any temperature: right out of the pan, warm, room temperature, or even straight from the refrigerator. For me its best, however, when it sits for at least an hour so its earthy taste fully develops.

1 large bunch broccoli
10 pitted black Mediterranean-style olives
$1/3$ cup crushed tomatoes in heavy puree
$1/4$ cup extra-virgin olive oil
$1/3$ cup red wine
1 tablespoon freshly grated Parmesan cheese

1 Cut off the large broccoli stems and save for another use. Cut enough of the head into 2- to $2\frac{1}{2}$-inch-wide florets to measure 2 quarts. Coarsely chop olives.

2 Gently mix broccoli, olives, tomatoes, olive oil, and red wine together in a large saucepan. Bring to a simmer over high heat, 1 to 2 minutes. Cover and reduce heat to low. Cook, stirring occasionally, until broccoli is tender, 18 to 20 minutes.

3 Stir in grated cheese and season with salt and pepper to taste.

4 SERVINGS

other ideas

VARIATIONS *Using a vegetable peeler, shave thin strips of Parmesan over the top right before serving and omit the grated cheese inside.*

Replace the crushed tomatoes with prepared tomato sauce or about 3 tablespoons of tomato puree.

Carrots with Olive Oil and Oregano

When whole garlic cloves are cooked in olive oil over low heat, they infuse the oil in a clear but gentle way with their flavor. The oil, along with a good sprinkle of oregano, dresses these carrots while they are still warm so they drink in the seasonings more readily. They're finished with a small squeeze of lemon juice, which brightens the taste without turning them into a salad. Served as is, they make a comforting side dish but they can also be an antipasto, with or without adding extra lemon juice.

2 $1/2$ tablespoons extra-virgin olive oil

2 large garlic cloves

1 pound carrots

$1/2$ teaspoon dried oregano

$3/4$ teaspoon freshly squeezed lemon juice

1 Warm olive oil in small skillet over low heat. Add garlic and cook, turning occasionally, until both sides are golden. Discard garlic. Set aside oil.

2 Bring a large saucepan of salted water to a boil over high heat. Peel and cut carrots into $1/2$-inch-thick rounds. Boil until tender, about 7 minutes. Drain well.

3 Transfer carrots to medium bowl. Toss with oregano, then oil. Toss with lemon juice and season with salt to taste. Serve hot, warm, or at room temperature.

4 SERVINGS

other ideas

VARIATIONS *For a pronounced garlic flavor, slip the cooked cloves into the dressed carrots and let the dish marinate overnight in the refrigerator.*

If you want to turn the carrots into a salad, add more lemon juice or a little vinegar. Then toss them, if you like, with cooked white beans and red onion for a good lunch or light supper. Big flakes of Italian tuna (the kind packed in olive oil) make a traditional and perfect garnish.

Eggplant with Red Onion and Tomato

Nice chunks of eggplant and thin slices of red onion simmer together in olive oil and crushed tomatoes until softly tender. The tomatoes are the bridge that pulls all the tastes together but the eggplant is definitely the star. This veggie dish is good served hot or at room temperature and could also be an antipasto.

1$^1/_2$ pounds eggplant
1 medium red onion
$^1/_4$ cup extra-virgin olive oil
$^1/_2$ cup crushed tomatoes in heavy puree

1   Trim ends from eggplant and discard. Cut into 1-inch dice. Thinly slice onion.

2   Mix olive oil in very large saucepan with crushed tomatoes over medium-low heat. Add eggplant and onion. Salt lightly and stir to combine. Cook until sound of sizzling starts, then cover. Cook, without stirring or removing cover, about 15 minutes. The vegetables will be cooked down by about one-half.

3 Remove cover and reduce heat to low. Stir up any brown residue stuck on pan bottom. Cook about 5 minutes more or until eggplant is tender, stirring occasionally. Season with salt and pepper to taste. Serve hot or at room temperature.

4 TO 5 SERVINGS

other ideas

SIMPLE TIPS *For safety sake before dicing, trim a thin slice off one of the eggplant's sides. Then lay the eggplant on the flat side to keep it from rolling and the knife from slipping as you cut.*

The brown residue that sticks to the pan adds flavor when stirred into the vegetables. However, it shouldn't be allowed to burn. If the pan is making frying, crackling sounds rather than moist, simmering sounds, lift the cover to check. Scrape up the bottom if it's browned, lower the heat, and finish cooking according to the recipe.

VARIATIONS *Cook a diced green or red bell pepper with the vegetables. With a chopped garlic clove, too, if you like.*

Serve the eggplant as is, as an antipasto, or stir in a few drops of red wine vinegar and/or some capers to taste. A sprinkle of fresh oregano leaves on top would be lovely.

Green Beans with Radicchio

Radicchio, the beautiful moon-shaped maroon lettuce from the chicory family, starts out with a bitter edge when raw. But after a short stint in the sauté pan, it sweetens and adds its graceful note of flavor to tender, supple green beans.

1 pound green beans
$3/4$ small head radicchio
2 tablespoons butter
1 medium garlic clove, minced
$1^1/2$ teaspoons freshly squeezed lemon juice

1   Bring a large saucepan of salted water to a boil over high heat. Snap off ends of beans. Core radicchio and finely slice. Blanch beans in water until just tender, 5 to 7 minutes. Drain well and reserve pan.

2   Return pan to medium heat and add butter. When melted, stir in radicchio and garlic. Cook, stirring occasionally, until lettuce is lightly wilted, about 3 minutes.

3 Reduce heat to low and stir in beans. Cook, stirring occasionally, until beans are very tender, about 2 minutes. Season with lemon juice and salt and pepper to taste. Serve hot.

4 SERVINGS

other ideas

SIMPLE TIP *There are a number of varieties of radicchio grown in Italy. Another we get here looks like a head of burgundy-colored Romaine lettuce. Use it just like the more familiar round one.*

Green Beans and Zucchini with Potatoes

This tender blend of green vegetables and potatoes couldn't be more comforting. And it just might be the only side dish dinner needs. Sometimes the vegetables brown a bit as they cook, making them all the better for that extra touch of flavor.

$1/2$ pound green beans

2 medium boiling potatoes

1 medium zucchini

3 tablespoons extra-virgin olive oil

$1/2$ teaspoon dried oregano

1 Bring a large saucepan of salted water to a boil over high heat for the beans. Snap ends off beans. Peel and thinly slice potatoes. Slice zucchini into thin rounds.

2 Add beans and potatoes to boiling water. Let water return to boil and boil vegetables 1 minute. Drain immediately.

3   Heat olive oil in a large skillet over medium heat. Stir in zucchini to coat with oil. Stir in beans and potatoes. Sprinkle with oregano. Cover and cook over low heat; you should hear gentle sizzling. Cook, stirring occasionally, until all the vegetables are tender, 8 to 10 minutes. Season with salt and pepper to taste and serve hot.

4 SERVINGS

Leeks Baked with Butter and Marjoram

With onionlike flavor but in a more genteel way, leeks are famous for what they can do for soup. But they have a lot to offer on their own as a side dish, too. For example, when baked in the oven with a little broth they become succulent and tender enough to cut with a fork. Then when their juices are boiled down with a few lumps of butter they thicken into a sauce and heighten the taste of the mild, sweet vegetable.

5 medium to large leeks (1 to 1$\frac{1}{4}$ inches in diameter)
$\frac{1}{8}$ teaspoon dried marjoram
1 cup chicken broth
1$\frac{1}{2}$ tablespoons cold butter, cut into 3 pieces
1 teaspoon chopped parsley

1 Preheat oven to 400°F. Trim roots of leeks, if necessary. Cut off dark green leaves and discard. Save remaining white and light green lengths. Cut each in half lengthwise. Fill very large bowl or sink with cold water and wash, spreading leaves open slightly. Drain well.

2 Lay snugly in 8- to 9-inch baking dish. Season lightly with salt and pepper, then with marjoram. Pour broth on top. Cover tightly with foil and bake until tender, 30 to 40

minutes. Transfer to serving dish and pour juices into small skillet. There should be about $1/2$ cup.

3 Boil juices down over high heat, adding any further from serving dish, until about 2 tablespoons remain, 5 to 8 minutes. Add cold butter and boil until thick, about 2 minutes. Pepper lightly; no further salt should be needed. Pour sauce over leeks, sprinkle with parsley, and serve.

4 SERVINGS

other ideas

SIMPLE TIP *Leeks are notoriously sandy inside. Trim off the dark green parts and split them lengthwise, being sure not to cut through the ends so the layers hold together. Cut once or twice again lengthwise to open them further. Soak in a large bowl of cold water for at least 5 minutes, swishing them around occasionally, to let the grit fall to the bottom.*

Sautéed Mushrooms with Garlic, Olive Oil, and Parsley

Mushrooms are favorite edibles in Italy, and there are many kinds in the markets to choose from come spring and fall. And while we can't always find the most interesting wild types here, creminis have good deep flavor and are widely available. And, of course, white button mushrooms are good, too. Traditionally sautéed with garlic, olive oil, and fresh parsley, these are seasoned with just enough garlic to satisfy the taste buds without overpowering the mushrooms.

1 pound cremini or white button mushrooms, or a mixture
2 garlic cloves
3 1/2 tablespoons extra-virgin olive oil
1 1/2 tablespoons minced parsley

1   Slice mushrooms about 1/4 inch thick. Mince garlic.

2   Warm olive oil in large skillet over medium heat. Add garlic and cook, stirring frequently, until it turns aromatic without coloring, 15 to 30 seconds. Stir in mushrooms and cook until juices flow, 4 to 5 minutes, stirring occasionally. Continue cooking until juices evaporate and mushrooms begin to fry, 2 to 3 minutes, stirring occasionally.

3 Remove skillet from heat and season with salt and pepper to taste. Stir in parsley and serve hot or warm.

4 TO 5 SERVINGS

other ideas

SIMPLE TIP *In open baskets of mushrooms you may find some that have aged and developed deeper flavor as a result. They will look darker in color and have visible gills because the caps have started to spread. They are excellent for cooking (but not for serving raw) as long as they feel dry to the touch and not sticky. Don't buy older mushrooms in tightly wrapped containers, though, because they need air to age well.*

DRESS IT UP *A mixture of chanterelle, oyster, and cremini mushrooms with a shiitake or two is an elegant and earthy combination. Portobellos are delicious too, but they can turn the other mushrooms black in color. For the most authentic flavor, include about $1/2$ ounce of reconstituted and chopped dried porcini mushrooms. For instructions on how to reconstitute, see Arborio Rice Pilaf with Porcini Mushrooms (pages 200–201).*

VARIATION *Use chopped fresh mint instead of parsley or half of each. Or substitute a generous 1 teaspoon dried mint for all the parsley.*

Spinach with Mascarpone

Cooked spinach turns silkily creamy when the soft and feather light Italian cream cheese, mascarpone, is stirred in. Even frozen spinach has the good vegetable taste of fresh when done this way. And it doubles, triples, or even quadruples perfectly if you'd like a bigger quantity. The recipe didn't start out as a vegetable side dish, though. It was my friends' family recipe for stuffing. To find out how the stuffing was made, see Variation.

One 10-ounce box chopped spinach, defrosted
1 1/2 tablespoons butter
2 tablespoons finely chopped red onion
1/3 cup mascarpone
2 tablespoons grated Parmesan cheese

1 Place spinach in colander in sink. Doing handfuls at a time, squeeze out and reserve 1/3 cup water. Squeeze out remaining water and discard.

2 Melt butter in medium skillet over low heat. Cook onion, stirring occasionally, until tender but not browned, 3 to 4 minutes. Add spinach with reserved water and cook until tender and moist but not runny, 4 to 5 minutes, stirring occasionally.

3   Stir in mascarpone until spinach is coated and hot, 1 to 2 minutes. Remove skillet from heat, stir in grated Parmesan, and season to taste with salt and pepper. Serve.

3 TO 4 SERVINGS

other ideas

SIMPLE TIP *If the spinach isn't defrosted when you want to make the dish, cook it about 2 minutes less than the package directions. Then drain it well. Stir it into the cooked red onion and proceed with the recipe. If it remains too wet, cook over higher heat a minute or so. If it's too dry, stir in a few tablespoons of hot water or broth before adding the mascarpone.*

VARIATION *This spinach is a variation of a recipe from Nonna Corti and the Zazzi family. For them, grandmother Corti multiplied the ingredients by 4 to make a stuffing for poultry. She used minced shallots instead of onion, however, and added chopped mushrooms to cook for just a minute or two before adding the spinach. The liquid from the mushrooms supplied the moisture. She finished the dish with mascarpone and grated Parmesan before letting it cool and stuffing the bird.*

Baked Spinach with Garlic Bread Crumbs

A small mountain of spinach is tossed in olive oil with a seasoning or two, then packed into a casserole and sprinkled with garlicky bread crumbs. Once in the oven, the spinach collapses into meltingly tender leaves under a smattering of golden, crisped bits. Spinach is cooked just this way in both Italy and in France, but sometimes it gets a good drizzle of olive oil only and no crumbs are used.

Two 9-ounce bags washed spinach
$1/4$ cup extra-virgin olive oil
Small pinch crushed red pepper flakes
3 tablespoons plain dry bread crumbs
1 large garlic clove, minced

1   Preheat oven to 400°F. Toss spinach in a very large bowl or pot with 3 tablespoons olive oil until leaves are lightly coated. Toss again with $1/8$ teaspoon salt, pinch of black pepper, and red pepper flakes. Mix bread crumbs with garlic and remaining 1 tablespoon olive oil in a small bowl. Season with salt and pepper to taste.

2   Pack spinach into a $2 1/2$-quart baking dish as best as possible; it will mound. Sprinkle prepared bread crumbs over top.

3   Bake until spinach fills casserole by about half, is very tender, and crumbs are golden brown, about 30 minutes. Serve hot.

6 SERVINGS

other ideas

SIMPLE TIPS *It's important to salt spinach lightly when it is raw because while it may look like a lot, once it's cooked it becomes a fraction of its former self!*

Don't have a large enough casserole? Then pack about half the spinach into a smaller dish and bake 10 minutes or so until the leaves begin to collapse. Then put in the rest and sprinkle with the bread crumbs.

Grilled Summer Squash with Parsley and Oregano

Both green and yellow squash have more taste, I think, when they've been cooked on the grill and gotten a little charred. Good as they are with merely a drizzle of olive oil and dash of salt and pepper, here is a more lively preparation that doesn't take a lot more effort: toss the just-cooked squash with chopped parsley and garlic, sprinkle with oregano, and add a splash of vinegar. Since the squash is warm and tender, it will drink in all the flavors. I'm hard pressed to decide if this should be called a side dish, salad, or antipasto, since it can qualify as all three.

6 sprigs flat-leaf parsley
1 medium garlic clove, thinly sliced
$1/2$ teaspoon dried oregano
4 medium summer squash (2 green and 2 yellow)
2 tablespoons extra-virgin olive oil
$2 1/2$ teaspoons red wine vinegar

1 Prepare a medium fire in the barbecue grill. Pick leaves from parsley sprigs. Push into a mound and top with garlic. Finely chop together. Transfer to small bowl and stir in

oregano. Trim and discard squash ends. Cut each squash lengthwise in half. Toss in large bowl with olive oil.

2 Place squash on grill cut side down. Reserve bowl with excess oil. Grill, turning once until browned on both sides and tender-firm, 8 to 10 minutes. Return to bowl and let cool until cool enough to handle.

3 Cut squash into $1/2$-inch-wide diagonal pieces. Return to bowl. Toss with vinegar to coat, then with parsley-garlic mixture. Season with salt and pepper to taste. Serve warm, room temperature, or slightly chilled.

4 SERVINGS

other ideas

SIMPLE TIPS *The freshest squash have bright-colored skin without any blemishes. And when squeezed, they feel firm and dense along their whole length. Small to medium squash taste the sweetest and have the fewest seeds.*

Using 1 bowl throughout for oiling, cooling, and seasoning the squash saves all the olive oil and cooked juices for the dressing and makes for easier cleanup.

Little New Potatoes with Lemon Zest

These days, I see charming little "creamer" potatoes more and more frequently in the market. What they are are the smallest of the red and white (and sometimes yellow) new potatoes. They are so naturally good that not much is needed after the basic boiling. Here, though, they are treated to a last minute roll in olive oil and butter with lots of fresh lemon zest. Then sent off to the table sprinkled with coarse salt.

1 pound "creamers" (1- to 1 1/2-inch new potatoes)
1 tablespoon extra-virgin olive oil
1 1/2 tablespoons butter
Grated zest from 1 1/2 lemons

1   Bring potatoes to a boil in a large saucepan of lightly salted water. Cook at a low boil over medium-low heat until just tender, 12 to 15 minutes. Do not overcook. Drain.

2   Return to pan over low heat to dry for 1 minute, rolling them in pan occasionally. Add olive oil, butter, and lemon zest. Season with pepper to taste. Heat 1 minute, rolling pan.

3 Transfer potatoes to serving dish. Sprinkle with coarse salt to taste and serve hot.

4 SERVINGS

other ideas

SIMPLE TIP *If tiny "creamers" aren't available, pick the smallest red or white new potato you can find. And be sure to choose ones of similar size so they cook at the same rate. And if they end up being closer to medium, then boil them and cut them in half before tossing with the seasonings.*

Baked Potatoes with Romano Cheese

Waxy potatoes are first boiled, then coarsely mashed with olive oil and grated cheese. Then they're enriched with an egg yolk, packed into a shallow dish, and popped into a hot oven just long enough for the little peaks on top to crust lightly and turn golden. They end up tasting moist and rich, a touch tangy, and with a texture that's sort of fluffy. But fluffy in that satisfying, toothsome way that a forkful of just-baked Idaho potato is when you bite into it.

4 medium boiling potatoes
$1/3$ cup extra-virgin olive oil
$1/3$ cup grated Romano cheese
1 egg yolk, lightly beaten

1 Preheat oven to 425°F with rack in top third. Bring a large saucepan of salted water to a boil. Peel and quarter potatoes. Lightly grease a shallow 1- to $1^1/_2$-quart baking dish with olive oil.

2 Cook potatoes at a medium boil until tender, 15 to 20 minutes. Drain, then return to cooking pot. Using a large spoon, coarsely mash while gradually adding olive oil. Stir in $1/_4$ cup of grated cheese. Remove pan from heat, season to taste with salt and pepper. Mix in egg yolk.

3 Pack into baking dish and make small swirls over top with the spoon. Sprinkle with remaining 1^1/$_3$ tablespoons cheese and bake until tipped with gold. Serve hot.

4 TO 6 SERVINGS

other ideas

VARIATION *For a slightly creamier, less hearty version, mash the potatoes with* ^{1}/$_4$ *cup softened butter instead of the olive oil and substitute* ^{1}/$_3$ *cup grated Parmesan for the Romano.*

Arborio Rice Pilaf with Porcini Mushrooms

Arborio rice is short-grain Italian rice used for making risotto, the rich rice dish that, like pasta, is its own course in an Italian meal. Risotto is made by gradually stirring small amounts of hot broth into the rice until it turns al dente and the broth thickens from the natural starch, surrounding the grains in luxurious creaminess. But when the rice is rinsed first and the liquid added all at once like a pilaf, well, it becomes one. But it is a pilaf with distinction because of the character of the rice itself. And because it is aromatic and woodsy tasting from porcini, the classic Italian fungi, and filled with the sweet and nutty notes of sage, red onion, and bay leaf.

1/4 cup dried porcini mushrooms (about 1/4 ounce)

1 medium red onion

3/4 cup Italian arborio rice

2 tablespoons butter

3/4 teaspoon rubbed dried sage

2 bay leaves

1   Soak porcini mushrooms covered with 1 1/4 cups hot water until softened, about 20

minutes. Finely chop onion. Rinse rice 4 or 5 times under cold running water until water looks clear. Drain well.

2 Lift mushrooms from soaking water. Save water and add additional water, if necessary, to bring back to 1¼ cups. Dry mushrooms on paper towels and trim off any hard or gritty parts. Finely chop.

3 Melt butter in medium saucepan over medium heat. Add mushrooms, onion, sage, and bay leaves. Cook, stirring occasionally, until onion begins to soften, about 3 minutes. Add rice and cook, stirring frequently, 2 minutes. Add soaking water and season with ¾ teaspoon salt. Bring to a boil, then immediately reduce heat to low. Cover and cook until rice is cooked and liquid absorbed, 18 minutes. Fluff grains with fork and serve hot.

4 SERVINGS

other ideas

SIMPLE TIPS *Dried porcini are sold in small cellophane or plastic packets. The best quality have nice large slices that are creamy beige in color. Avoid packages consisting of small, dark pieces as they're likely to be gritty and have a lot of waste.*

Arborio is the most common variety of short-grain Italian rice available here. However, any of the other varieties, such as carnaroli or vialone nano, will work just as well.

Lifting the reconstituted porcini out of the soaking water lets any grit stay on the bottom of the bowl so when you add the water to the rice you can avoid adding the grit.

VARIATIONS *Bake the pilaf in a preheated 350°F oven instead of cooking it on top of the stove.*

Substitute a cup of finely chopped cremini, portobello, or regular white mushrooms for the porcini. Sauté them with the onion and seasonings until their liquid has evaporated and use chicken or vegetable broth in place of the mushroom soaking water.

the simpler the better Desserts

Baked Apples with Amaretti Cookies and Mascarpone   204

Chocolate Marsala Cake   206

Espresso Cream   208

Figs with Orange and Basil   210

Ginger Pine Nut Cookies   212

"Drowned" Ice Cream   214

Lemon Granita   216

Peaches in Red Wine with Almonds   218

Fresh Ricotta with Fruit   220

Balsamic Vinegar–Glazed Strawberries   222

Baked Apples with Amaretti Cookies and Mascarpone

This dessert is warming and comforting, just like baked apples are supposed to be. But these apples also manage to be sophisticated at the same time. That's thanks to the addition of slightly bitter almond cookies, Italian amaretti, and rich buttery mascarpone, which together add a touch of refinement. The mascarpone is used as both a binder for the cookie crumb filling and a topping for the hot apples. Gala apples, with their pleasant balance of tart and sweet, are a good choice here because they hold their shape well during baking and are just the right size for a single serving.

1 lemon

4 Gala apples, 7 to 8 ounces each

$^3/_4$ cup amaretti cookie crumbs

One $8^1/_2$-ounce container mascarpone cheese

1 cup apple cider

1 Preheat oven to 400°F. Cut lemon in half. Working with 1 apple at a time, remove peel halfway down apple with vegetable peeler. Using a melon baller, scoop out most of core, going almost, but not quite, to the bottom. Rub peeled part of apple with lemon half to prevent discoloration and squeeze a little juice into cored area.

2 Mix amaretti crumbs with 2 tablespoons mascarpone in a small bowl until well combined and malleable. Pack cored area of each apple with one-fourth of crumb mixture. Place apples in buttered 8-inch square baking pan. Pour cider around apples. Cover with buttered aluminum foil, buttered side down.

3 Bake 45 minutes. Remove foil. Continue baking, basting occasionally with juices in pan, until apples are barely tender when pierced with tip of a knife, about 15 minutes. Place warm apples with their juices in soup bowls. Top each with a dollop of mascarpone and serve right away.

4 SERVINGS

other ideas

SIMPLE TIPS *Amaretti are crisp, dry cookies that get their distinctive flavor from bitter almonds. These days they are often carried in supermarkets. But if yours does not, they can always be found in Italian delicatessens, as well as other specialty grocers. They come packed in both pretty red tins and bags.*

To make crumbs, place the amaretti cookies in a mini-food processor and process until they are small crumbs. Or lay the cookies between sheets of plastic wrap and crush them with a rolling pin.

VARIATIONS *If you can't find amaretti, there are other cookie possibilities. Biscotti, particularly almond, will work well. Gingersnaps or vanilla wafers aren't Italian, but they'll taste delicious nonetheless.*

Use apple juice in place of apple cider.

Drizzle apples with 2 tablespoons almond-flavored liqueur, such as Amaretto di Sarrono, before covering them with foil and baking.

Chocolate Marsala Cake

This rich chocolate cake with its slightly creamy center has a good amount of Marsala baked in it. And while you don't taste the wine as wine when you eat the cake, its presence contributes character. Baking the cake is a little different, too: it's underbaked. Consider it done when a pick inserted in the middle still has batter clinging to it. Melting the chocolate is also simplified; no double boiler or microwave needed. Simply melt the chocolate in a low oven with a close eye kept on it so it doesn't scorch. All said and done, thin wedges of this unusual cake are lovely at teatime and generous wedges an anytime treat.

6 ounces bittersweet chocolate, chopped

$1/3$ cup dry Marsala wine

$1/3$ cup mascarpone cheese

4 eggs, at room temperature

1 cup sugar

$3/4$ cup flour

1   Preheat oven to 300°F with rack in center. Grease an 8 x 2-inch round cake pan with oil. Line bottom with round of waxed paper. Oil paper. Melt chocolate in small saucepan in oven, 3 to 5 minutes. Remove, stir until smooth, and let cool. Increase oven temperature to 350°F.

2 Gradually stir Marsala into mascarpone in small bowl until smooth. Gradually add mascarpone mixture to chocolate until smooth. Using standing mixer with whip attachment or handheld electric beaters, whip eggs with sugar until pale, tripled in volume, and whip leaves dissolving tracks, about 3 minutes. Reduce speed to low and add flour in 4 parts alternating with chocolate-mascarpone in 3, beginning and ending with flour and until no streaks can be seen, 2 to 3 minutes. Stir in $1/8$ teaspoon salt. Transfer batter to prepared pan.

3 Bake until batter clinging to wooden pick inserted in center feels slightly sticky and top has several cracks, about 35 minutes. Remove from oven. Run paring knife around top $1/2$ inch to release edge. Cool on rack 10 minutes. Sandwich pan with second rack and flip. Carefully lift off pan. Sandwich cake with rack and turn right side up. Let cool completely. Serve cut in wedges.

8 TO 10 SERVINGS

other ideas

SIMPLE TIPS *Bring eggs to room temperature quickly by placing them in a bowl of very warm, but not hot, water.*

To measure flour accurately, first stir it in its container. Then place a nesting type measuring cup on a sheet of waxed paper. Spoon the flour into the cup to overflowing and do not shake or shift the cup. Finally, sweep across the top with a long straight-edged tool such as a chopstick or metal spatula.

DRESS IT UP *Dust the top of the cake with confectioners' sugar.*

Serve the wedges with a big dollop of unsweetened whipped cream garnished with ripe pear slices.

Espresso Cream

Silken and light, this dessert cream is infused with the special taste of espresso without its potent kick. Spoonfuls are like bites of a coffee cloud, not sips from a powerhouse in a cup. It's lovely served with any sort of crisp cookie, but chocolate biscotti is great. For this recipe it's important that the ricotta be on the dry side. To be sure of that, see Simple Tip before beginning.

1$^3/_4$ teaspoons instant espresso powder

$^3/_4$ cup ricotta cheese, preferably fresh ricotta, drained if necessary

$^1/_4$ cup mascarpone cheese

$^1/_3$ cup confectioners' sugar

$^3/_4$ cup heavy cream

1   Boil $^1/_4$ cup water in a small saucepan. Remove from heat and stir in espresso powder. Let cool.

2   Puree ricotta and mascarpone cheeses with sugar in food processor until very smooth, about 2 minutes. Gradually add 3 tablespoons brewed espresso, then transfer mixture to large bowl. Discard remaining espresso.

3 Without washing processor bowl, process cream until mounds form, about 1 minute. Stir half of whipped cream into ricotta mixture until smooth. Fold in remaining until no streaks can be seen. Spoon into bowls. Serve right away or chill before serving.

4 TO 5 SERVINGS

other ideas

SIMPLE TIP *Fresh ricotta in a plastic draining basket can be found at Italian delicatessens and cheese stores. It's important that the ricotta be somewhat dry or the finished Espresso Cream may be loose. If the ricotta is like very moist cottage cheese, transfer it to a cheesecloth-lined strainer set over a bowl and refrigerate for at least 3 hours or, better yet, overnight before using. The ricotta should lose between 1 and 2 tablespoons liquid during that time.*

DRESS IT UP *Sprinkle the servings with grated dark chocolate or a few chocolate coffee beans.*

Divide 1/2 cup of small Italian amaretti cookies, or other cookie, over the bottom of individual bowls. Spoon the cream over them and chill 30 to 40 minutes. Sprinkle with grated chocolate or chocolate coffee beans when serving, if you like.

VARIATION *Serve dollops of the Espresso Cream alongside or on top of the Chocolate Marsala Cake (page 206).*

Figs with Orange and Basil

This recipe originated with the great British food writer Elizabeth David, from her book *Mediterranean Food.* In it, she spoke of lushly ripe figs macerated in the juice of oranges: 2 perfect fruits in simple harmony. Here, I've taken the liberty of adding a touch of sour cream and fresh basil just in case our supermarket figs are not as voluptuous as we hope they'd be.

1 1/2 tablespoons slivered almonds

6 small sprigs fresh basil

1 1/2 tablespoons sour cream

3/4 cup freshly squeezed orange juice

8 ripe black or green figs

1   Preheat oven to 350°F (or use a toaster oven). Toast almonds in a baking pan until golden, 6 to 8 minutes. Let cool. Pick leaves from 2 basil sprigs and tear into small pieces.

2   Place sour cream in a large bowl and gradually stir in orange juice until smooth and creamy. Rinse and dry figs on paper towels, then trim off stems. Cut figs into quarters and add to bowl with torn basil. Fold together gently with rubber spatula. Cover and refrigerate for 15 minutes to combine flavors.

3 Gently stir figs, then spoon into bowls. Sprinkle with almonds, garnish with a basil sprig, and serve.

4 SERVINGS

other ideas

SIMPLE TIP *If the orange–sour cream sauce seems a little tart, stir in a teaspoon or two of superfine, instant-dissolving sugar.*

Ginger Pine Nut Cookies

The presence of olive oil in baked goods and pastries is common in Mediterranean countries, where it's put to excellent use creating good textures and enhancing flavors without leaving its own telltale taste. These crisp cookies—a result of the olive oil—are also nicely flavored with ginger, a pinch of cinnamon, and a generous amount of buttery pine nuts. You might not think of the spices as being genuine to Italian cuisine, but they arrived in Italy via Venice during its glorious spice trade years.

1 cup all-purpose flour

$2/3$ cup sugar

2 teaspoons ground ginger

$1/4$ teaspoon ground cinnamon

1 teaspoon baking soda

$2/3$ cup pine nuts

1 egg, at room temperature

$1/4$ cup olive oil

1   Preheat oven to 350°F with rack in center. Place flour, sugar, ginger, cinnamon, baking soda, and $1/4$ teaspoon salt in a medium bowl. Combine well with a whisk. Stir in pine nuts.

2 Break egg into large bowl and beat in olive oil with a fork until lightly thickens, about 30 seconds. Gradually add dry ingredients, mixing entire time with fork. When all dry ingredients are added, dough should be moist and smooth and studded with nuts. Pinch off pieces of dough and roll into 1-inch balls. Set about 2 inches apart on parchment-lined cookie sheets or nonstick sheets.

3 Bake until tops begin to crack and bottoms are very pale gold, about 10 minutes. The tops will feel slightly soft when pressed. Transfer cookies to rack to cool.

ABOUT THIRTY-FOUR 2^1/$_2$-INCH COOKIES

other ideas

SIMPLE TIP *To measure flour accurately, first stir it in its container to aerate it. Then place a nesting-type measuring cup on a sheet of waxed paper. Spoon the flour into the cup to overflowing and do not shake or shift the cup. Finally, sweep across the top with a long straight-edged tool such as a chopstick or metal spatula.*

VARIATIONS *For a crisp texture throughout, bake the cookies an additional 2 minutes.*

Make marmalade cookie sandwiches: For each cookie, spread about ^{3}/$_4$ teaspoon ginger, lemon, or orange marmalade over the flat bottom of a cooled cookie. Then press the bottom of another cookie against the jam. Continue sandwiching all the cookies in the same fashion.

"Drowned" Ice Cream

You will find this refreshing—and stimulating—combination of brewed espresso and gelato at cafés all over Italy, where it is called *café affogato* (drowned coffee). It is simplicity personified, but don't feel you need an expensive electric pressure-operated espresso maker to make it at home. You can prepare a strong pot of Italian-roast coffee (for the proper full-bodied flavor) in a drip coffee maker, or cook up a batch of espresso in an inexpensive *moka* or *Napoletana* pot on top of the stove. In hot weather, you may want to chill the coffee first so the ice cream doesn't melt so quickly.

1 quart vanilla gelato or ice cream
1 cup brewed Italian-roast coffee or espresso (either hot, cooled to room temperature, or chilled)

1   For each serving, place a large scoop of ice cream (about 1 cup) in a wine glass.

2   Pour ¼ cup coffee around the ice cream.

3   Serve immediately.

4 SERVINGS

SIMPLE TIP *Gelato is simply Italian-style ice cream. It's made with lots of egg yolks and the freshest cream, which often makes it richer and lusher than our American counterpart. Either ice cream or gelato, though, will be great in your* café affogato.

VARIATIONS *Substitute your favorite flavor of ice cream for the vanilla.*

Match the ice cream with an appropriate spirit, such as hazelnut ice cream with Frangelico, toasted almond with Amaretto, or chocolate with rum. Pour about 1 tablespoon liquor over each serving at the end.

A big spoonful of whipped cream over each serving is gilding the lily, but if you have cream around, why not go for it? But try to resist the desire to add chocolate syrup, sprinkles, nuts, or the like, which would turn it into an American sundae.

Lemon Granita

Making homemade ice cream is never really a simple project, but homemade granita couldn't be easier. Granita can be prepared right in your freezer without an ice cream machine. Slushy and refreshing like sorbet, though with a texture a bit more coarse, lemon granita is one of the most invigorating desserts around, and perfect for a hot summer night.

4 to 5 large lemons
1 cup sugar

1 Place a 9 x 13-inch metal baking pan in freezer. Grate zest from 2 lemons; set aside. Squeeze juice from remaining lemons, reserving seeds. You should have $3/4$ cup juice with seeds. Process juice and seeds, sugar, and 3 cups water in blender to pulverize seeds and dissolve sugar. Strain into bowl, then stir in lemon zest. Pour into chilled pan. Return pan to freezer.

2 Freeze until ice crystals form around edges of lemon mixture, about 1 hour. Stir crystals back into mixture with a slotted metal spoon. Freeze again until more crystals form. Stir again, breaking up semifrozen mixture with spoon. Continue freezing and stirring until granita is frozen into a slush, about 3 hours total.

3 Spoon granita into chilled individual dessert bowls or stemmed glasses. Serve right away.

other ideas

SIMPLE TIPS *The basic lemon syrup will taste quite sugary but don't be alarmed; chilling and freezing dulls the sweetness.*

Grappa is a strong, clear spirit distilled from grape pressings left from wine making. There is very expensive, fine grappa (bottled in crystal), but unless you count yourself as a grappa aficionado, a moderately priced brand will do just fine.

If not serving the granita right away, then freeze it in a covered container. When ready to serve, let it sit at room temperature for a few minutes, then process it in a food processor until it turns to slush.

VARIATIONS *Sprinkle each serving with a tablespoon of grappa or with vodka. Vodka itself has less flavor than grappa, but they both heighten the lemon flavor of the granita in the same way.*

Sprinkle the granita with fresh berries such as blueberries, blackberries, or raspberries when serving.

Peaches in Red Wine with Almonds

I can't imagine a more gently sophisticated, refreshing dessert for a summer's evening than these ripe peaches adrift in a shallow pool of lightly sweetened red wine. And when you slip a wedge into your mouth, you'll find that the peach's sweet purity has absorbed a touch of the grape's complexity. Once the fruit is all gone, all that's left is to pick up the glass and drink the wine down.

2 tablespoons sliced almonds

1 cup Chianti, Montepulciano, or other red wine

1 tablespoon sugar

4 large ripe peaches

1   Preheat the oven to 350°F (or use a toaster oven). Toast almonds on a baking pan until golden, 6 to 8 minutes. Remove and let cool. Combine wine with sugar and stir to dissolve. Bring a large saucepan of water to a boil for the peaches.

2   With a paring knife, cut a shallow "x" into each peach opposite its stem end. Doing 1 or 2 at a time, drop into boiling water for 10 seconds. Remove immediately and repeat with rest. Peel off skin starting from "x." Slice into thin wedges directly into stemmed glasses or serving bowl.

3   Pour sweetened wine over peach slices and let sit 5 to 10 minutes. Sprinkle with toasted almonds and serve.

4 SERVINGS

other ideas

SIMPLE TIP *A peach must be ripe in order to peel it using the 10-second dip in boiling water method. Though sometimes it does need another second or two beyond the first 10 seconds. But if it doesn't peel, it isn't ripe and you're just cooking them.*

DRESS IT UP *Serve a plate of biscotti alongside.*

Fresh Ricotta with Fruit

The milky taste of ricotta cheese is delightfully delicate, and if it's your sort of thing, a real pleasure to just eat out of the bowl. In Italy it's made from ewe's milk, though here from cow's. But either way, the fresher it is, the better. Nothing more than lightly sweetened ricotta highlighted with a pinch of spice and served with luscious fruit, this utterly simple dessert makes a charming end to a meal. Serve it in the summer with berries, melon, apricots, peaches, nectarines, or figs. And in the fall and winter with plums, pears, kiwi, or orange or tangerine segments. Or combine a number of fruit any time of year.

1^1/$_3$ cups ricotta cheese, preferably fresh ricotta

4 to 6 tablespoons milk

1 tablespoon sugar, or to taste

^{1}/$_4$ teaspoon vanilla extract

Grated nutmeg

3 cups berries, diced melon, pears, or other fruit

1 Place ricotta in medium bowl. Gradually stir in enough milk to make cheese creamy and a little looser but not runny. Stir in sugar and vanilla.

2   Spoon ricotta into center of plates. Sprinkle with nutmeg.

3   Surround ricotta with fruit and serve.

4 SERVINGS

other ideas

SIMPLE TIP *Some ricotta is drier than others because it has been drained of some or much of its liquid. If the kind you have is quite moist and creamy, add the milk very gradually as it may not need much.*

DRESS IT UP *Serving just a few kinds of fruit, as well as how they're cut, can make the dessert appear more deluxe. For instance, a combination of blackberries and raspberries makes a striking presentation. Or thin, alternating slices of fresh fig and melon look more elegant than if diced.*

VARIATIONS *Sprinkle the ricotta with cinnamon instead of nutmeg.*

Scatter some chopped toasted walnuts or hazelnuts over the dish.

Surround the ricotta with sliced strawberries and drizzle with balsamic vinegar.

Balsamic Vinegar–Glazed Strawberries

Italians love fruit for dessert savored naturally. And sometimes enhanced with just a drop or two or splash of something that adds a discrete yet distinct note. Fresh strawberries drizzled with aged balsamic vinegar is one of the favorites. Taking the idea a step further, these berries are gently rolled in a hot pan with butter, sugar, and vinegar. After just seconds, they are coated in a delicate glaze with a hint of the sweet balsamic. They are delightful served right out of the pan, but not bad, too, over a scoop of gelato or ice cream!

3 cups fresh strawberries
2 tablespoons unsalted butter
2 tablespoons sugar
2 teaspoons balsamic vinegar

1   Rinse strawberries. Dry with paper towels, then hull. If small, leave whole, otherwise cut into halves or quarters.

2   Melt butter with sugar in a large skillet over medium heat, stirring, about 1 minute. Add vinegar and stir until smooth and color evens out, about 15 seconds.

3 Remove pan from heat and add berries. Stir to coat and serve immediately.

4 SERVINGS

other ideas

DRESS IT UP *Spoon the berries over a scoop of pistachio, vanilla, chocolate, or peach gelato or ice cream. Stick in a crunchy cookie, too, if you want.*

Index

A

Almonds, Peaches in Red Wine
with, 218–219
Amaretti Cookies
to crumb, 205
and Mascarpone, Baked Apples
with, 204–205
Anchovy(ies)
in Basil and Olive Oil Dip, 4–5
Butter, Shrimp with, 82–83
in Castellane with Eggplant,
36–37
in Pot Roast with Red Wine,

Italian-Style, 130–131
in Risotto Puttanesca (variation),
69–70
Antipasti, 2–17
Asparagus with Orange and
Parmesan Shavings, 2–3
Bruschetta, Roasted Eggplant,
6–7
Dip, Basil and Olive Oil, 4–5
Goat Cheese with Grapes and
Balsamic Vinegar, 8–9
ideas for, 16–17
Pizza Bread, Rosemary-Pepper,
10–11

Shrimp with Lemon and Garlic,
12–13
Zucchini with Lemon, 14–15
Apples, Baked, with Amaretti
Cookies and Mascarpone,
204–205
Arborio Rice Pilaf with Porcini
Mushrooms, 200–202
Artichoke(s)
as antipasti, 17
frozen, 173
Hearts with Onion, Balsamic
Vinegar, and Parmesan
Cheese, 172–173

Arugula
  and Basil Salad, 152–153
  Blood Orange, and Fennel Salad,
    154–155
Asparagus
  with Orange and Parmesan
    Shavings, 2–3
  Risotto, and Golden Garlic
    (variation), 67
  Sautéed, with Onion and Mint,
    174–175
  and Shrimp with Anchovy
    Butter (variation), 83

B

Balsamic (Vinegar)
  Artichoke Hearts with Onion,
    Parmesan and, 172–173
  Chicken Legs, Roast, with
    Tomato and, 112–113
  Goat Cheese with Grapes, 8–9
  Onions, Honey, Calf's Liver with,
    148–149
  Strawberries, -Glazed, 222–223

Basil
  and Arugula Salad, 152–153
  Bass, Sautéed, with Fresh
    Tomatoes and, 92–94
  in Black Olive Pesto, Potato
    Gnocchi with, 58–59
  Figs with Orange and, 210–211
  and Olive Oil Dip, 4–5
  Sweet Pepper, Tomato, and
    Onion Salad with, Summer,
    162–163
  Tomato, and Bread Soup, 30–31
Bass, Sautéed, with Fresh
    Tomatoes and Basil, 92–93
Bean(s). See Cannellini Bean(s);
    Green Beans
Beef
  Meatballs in Red Sauce,
    Old-Fashioned, 128–129
  meat broth, to dress up, 33
  Patties with Red Wine and
    Provolone, 122–123
  Pot Roast with Red Wine, Italian
    Style, 130
  Ragù, Red Wine, Mini-Rigatoni
    with, 50–51

Steak, Grilled, Tuscan-Style,
    124–125
  Steak with Red Wine, Olives,
    and Peperoncini, 126–127
Beet(s)
  to peel, 157
  Salad, Green Salad with
    (variation), 157
  Shredded, and Gorgonzola
    Salad, 156–157
Bell Pepper(s). See Pepper(s),
    Sweet Bread, Pizza,
    Rosemary-Pepper, 10–11
Bread Crumbs
  Garlic, Baked Spinach with,
    192–193
  Sautéed, Gemelli with Black
    Olives, Capers and, 42–43
Bread Soup
  Fontina and, 22–23
  Tomato, Basil and, 30–31
Broccoli with Black Olives and
    Red Wine, 176–177
Broth, meat, to dress up, 33
Bruschetta
  Roasted Eggplant, 6–7

topppings for, 17

Butter

    Anchovy, Shrimp with,
82–83

    Leeks, Baked with Marjoram
and, 186–187

    Linguine, Fresh, with Parmesan
Cheese, Mushrooms and,
46–47

    Potato Gnocchi, with Tomato,
Sage and, 60–61

    to soften, 47

C

Cabbage and Golden Garlic
Risotto, 66–67

Cake, Chocolate Marsala,
206–207

Calamari, Seafood Salad with
Mint and Scallion, 168–169

Calf's Liver with Balsamic Honey
Onions, 148–149

Cannellini Bean(s)

    as antipasti, 17

and Escarole Soup (variation),
19

and Prosciutto Soup, 20–21

Sausages with Tomatoes and,
140–141

Capers

    Chicken Fricassea with, 104–105

    Gemelli with Black Olives,
Sautéed Bread Crumbs and,
42–43

    in Risotto Puttanesca (variation),
69–70

    Sea Scallops, Oven-Roasted,
with White Wine and, 80–81

Carrot(s)

    with Olive Oil and Oregano,
178–179

    Risotto, and Golden Garlic
(variation), 67

    Salad (variation), 179

Castellane with Eggplant, 36–37

Cauliflower Salad, Tossed, 158–159

Chard, in Green Beans and Greens
Soup, 24–25

Cheese

    Goat Cheese with Grapes and

Balsamic Vinegar, 8–9

    Polenta with Walnuts and,
62–63

    Provolone, Beef Patties with
Red Wine and, 122–123

    See also Fontina; Gorgonzola;
Mascarpone; Mozzarella;
Parmesan; Ricotta; Romano
Cheese

Chicken

    breast, to slice horizontally, 107

    Breasts in Lemon and Egg Sauce,
100–101

    Breasts with Pancetta and Sage,
108–109

    Cacciatore, 96–97

    Cutlets in Garlic Cream,
102–103

    Diavolo, 98–99

    Fricassea with Capers, 104–105

    Legs, Roast, with Balsamic
Vinegar and Tomato, 112–113

    Marsala with Mushrooms,
106–107

    with Rosemary Sauce, 114–115

    Valdostana, 110–111

Chickpea(s)
  as antipasti, 17
  and Escarole Soup, 18–19
Chocolate Marsala Cake,
    206–207
Clams
  to clean, 73
  Steamed, with Garlic and Olive
    Oil, 72–73
Cod Fillets with Roasted Sweet
    Peppers, 74–75
Coffee. See Espresso
Cookies
  Ginger Pine Nut, 212–213
  Marmalade Sandwich (variation),
    213
Cream
  Espresso, 208–209
  Garlic, Chicken Cutlets in,
    102–103
  Lemon, Veal Chops with
    Hazelnuts and, 144–145
  Rosemary Tomato, Spaghetti
    with, 52–53

D

Desserts, 203–223
  Apples, Baked, with Amaretti
    Cookies and Mascarpone,
    204–205
  Cake, Chocolate Marsala,
    206–207
  Cookies, Ginger Pine Nut,
    212–213
  Cookies, Marmalade Sandwich
    (variation), 213
  Espresso Cream, 208–209
  Figs with Orange and Basil,
    210–211
  Granita, Lemon, 216–217
  Ice Cream, "Drowned", 214–215
  Peaches in Red Wine with
    Almonds, 218–219
  Ricotta, Fresh, with Fruit,
    220–221
  Strawberries, Balsamic
    Vinegar-Glazed, 222–223
  Dip, Basil and Olive Oil, 4–5
  "Drowned" Ice Cream, 214–215

E

Egg and Lemon Sauce, Chicken
    Breasts in, 100–101
Eggplant
  Bruschetta, Roasted, 6–7
  Castellane with, 36–37
  to dice, 37, 181
  with Red Onion and Tomato,
    180–181
Escarole and Chickpea Soup,
    18–19
Espresso
  Cream, 208–209
  Ice Cream, "Drowned",
    214–215

F

Fennel, Arugula, and Blood
    Orange Salad, 154–155
Fettuccine
  Fresh, with Sweet Red Onions
    and Walnuts, 38–39
  with Peas and Pancetta, 40–41

Figs with Orange and Basil, 210–211

Fish
as antipasti, 17
Bass, Sautéed, with Fresh Tomatoes and Basil, 92–94
Cod Fillets with Roasted Sweet Peppers, 74–75
fillets, to sauté, 93
Flounder, Crisp Crusted, 76–77
Sole with Parmesan Glaze, 86–87
Swordfish, Roman, 88–89
See also Anchovy(ies); Tuna

Flounder, Crisp Crusted, 76–77
Flour, to measure, 207, 213

Fontina
and Bread Soup, 22–23
in Chicken Valdostana, 110–111

Fruit
Ricotta, Fresh, with, 220–221
See also specific fruits

G

Garlic
Bread Crumbs, Baked Spinach with, 192–193
Clams, Steamed, with Olive Oil and, 72–73
Chicken Cutlets in Cream, 102–103
Crisp, Tuna, Sautéed, with Black Olives and, 90–91
Golden, and Cabbage Risotto, 66–67
Lamb Stew with Tomatoes, Rosemary and, 134–135
Mushrooms, Sautéed, with Olive Oil, Parsley and, 188–189
Onion, and Tomato, Shrimp with, 84–85
Shrimp with Lemon and, 12–13
slivers, to cut, 43
Veal Scallopini with Lemon, Bay and, 148–149

Gelato, "Drowned" Ice Cream, 214–215

Gemelli with Black Olives, Capers, and Sautéed Bread Crumbs, 42–43

Ginger Pine Nut Cookies, 212–213

Gnocchi, Potato
with Black Olive Pesto, 58–59
with Butter, Tomato, and Sage, 60–61
vacuum-packed, 61

Goat Cheese with Grapes and Balsamic Vinegar, 8–9

Gorgonzola
Pasta with Pine Nuts, Marie's, 44–45
and Shredded Beet Salad, 156–157

Granita, Lemon, 216–217

Grapes, Goat Cheese with Balsamic Vinegar and, 8–9

Grape Tomatoes, Spaghetti with Pesto and, 56–57

Green Beans
and Greens Soup, 24–25
with Radicchio, 182–183
and Zucchini with Potatoes, 184–185

Greens, and Green Beans Soup, 24–25

H

Hazelnuts, Veal Chops with Lemon Cream and, 144–145

I

Ice Cream, "Drowned", 214–215

L

Lamb
   Steaks with Mint Pesto, 132–133
   Stew with Garlic, Tomatoes, and Rosemary, 134–135
   stew meat, 135
Leeks
   Baked with Butter and Marjoram, 186–187
   to clean, 187

Lemon
   Chicken with Rosemary Sauce, 114–115
   Cream, Veal Chops with Hazelnuts and, 144–145
   and Egg Sauce, Chicken Breasts in, 100–101
   Granita, 216–217
   Shrimp with Garlic and, 12–13
   Turkey Piccata with Mozzarella, 116–117
   Veal Scallopini with Garlic, Bay and, 146–147
   Zest, Little New Potatoes with, 196–197
   Zucchini with, 14–15
Lentil and Spinach Soup, Puree of, 26–27
Linguine, Fresh, with Butter, Parmesan Cheese, and Mushrooms, 46–47
Liver, Calf's, with Balsamic Honey Onions, 148–149

M

Marie's Gorgonzola Pasta with Pine Nuts, 44–45
Marjoram
   Leeks Baked with Butter and, 186–187
   Turkey Breast, Roast, with Potatoes, Sage and, 118–119
Marsala
   Chicken, with Mushrooms, 106–107
   Chocolate Cake, 206–207
   Pork Chops Braised with, 138–139
Mascarpone
   and Amaretti Cookies, Baked Apples with, 204–205
   in Chocolate Marsala Cake, 206–207
   Spinach with, 190–191
Meatballs in Red Sauce, Old-Fashioned, 128–129
Meat broth, to dress up, 33
Mesclun Salad with Ricotta and Pine Nuts, 160–161

Mint
    Asparagus, Sautéed, with Onion
        and, 174–175
    Pesto, Lamb Steaks with,
        132–133
    Seafood Salad with Scallion
        and, 168–169
Mozzarella
    in Meatballs in Red Sauce,
        Old-Fashioned (variation),
        129
    Turkey Piccata with, 116–117
Mushrooms
    aged, 189
    as antipasti, 17
    in Chicken Cacciatore, 96–97
    Chicken Marsala with, 106–107
    dried, 201
    Linguine, Fresh, with Butter,
        Parmesan Cheese and,
        46–47
    mixtures of, 189
    Porcini, Arborio Rice Pilaf with,
        200–202
    Sautéed, with Garlic, Olive Oil,
        and Parsley, 188–189

Mussels
    Seafood Salad with Mint and
        Scallion (variation), 169
    Steamed with Tomatoes and
        Vegetables, 78–79

O

Olive(s)
    Black, Broccoli with Red Wine
        and, 176–177
    Black, Gemelli with Capers,
        Sautéed Bread Crumbs and,
        42–43
    Black, Pesto, Potato Gnocchi
        with, 58–59
    Black, Tuna, Sautéed, with Crisp
        Garlic and, 90–91
    to pit, 43
    in Risotto Puttanesca (variation),
        69–70
    Steak with Red Wine,
        Peperoncini and, 126–127
Olive Oil
    and Basil Dip, 4–5

Carrots with Oregano and,
        178–179
    Clams, Steamed, with Garlic
        and, 72–73
    Mushrooms, Sautéed, with
        Garlic, Parsley and, 188–189
Onion(s)
    Artichoke Hearts with Balsamic
        Vinegar, Parmesan and,
        172–173
    Asparagus, Sautéed, with Mint
        and, 174–175
    Balsamic Honey, Calf's Liver
        with, 148–149
    Garlic, and Tomato, Shrimp
        with, 84–85
    Red, Eggplant with Tomato and,
        180–181
    Red, Sweet, Fresh Fettuccine
        with Walnuts and, 38–39
    Sweet Pepper, and Tomato
        Salad with Basil, Summer,
        162–163
Orange(s)
    Asparagus with Parmesan
        Shavings and, 2–3

Blood, Arugula, and Fennel
Salad, 154–155
Figs with Basil and, 210–211
to slice, 155
Orechiette with Sausage and
Sweet Red Peppers, 48–49
Oregano
Carrots with Olive Oil and,
178–179
Summer Squash, Grilled, with
Parsley and, 194–195

P

Pancetta
Chicken Breasts with Sage and,
108–109
to cut and cook, 41
Fettuccine with Peas and, 40–41
Parmesan
Artichoke Hearts with Onion,
Balsamic Vinegar and,
172–173
Glaze, Sole with, 86–87
Linguine, Fresh, with Butter,

Mushrooms and, 46–47
Shavings, Asparagus, with
Orange and, 2–3
Parsley
Green Dressing, Rice Salad with,
166–167
Mushrooms, Sautéed, with
Garlic, Olive Oil and,
188–189
Summer Squash, Grilled, with
Oregano and, 194–195
Pasta, 36–57
Castellane with Eggplant, 36–37
Fettuccine, Fresh, with Sweet
Red Onions and Walnuts,
38–39
Fettuccine with Peas and
Pancetta, 40–41
Gemelli with Black Olives,
Capers, and Sautéed Bread
Crumbs, 42–43
Gorgonzola, with Pine Nuts,
Marie's, 44–45
Linguine, Fresh, with Butter,
Parmesan Cheese, and
Mushrooms, 46–47

Orechiette with Sausage and
Sweet Red Peppers, 48–49
Rigatoni, Mini-, with Red Wine
Ragù, 50–51
Spaghetti with Grape Tomatoes
and Pesto, 56–57
Spaghetti, Peppery, with
Romano Cheese, 54–55
Spaghetti with Rosemary
Tomato Cream, 52–53
Tortellini en Brodo, 32–33
Peaches
to peel, 219
in Red Wine with Almonds,
218–219
Peas, Fettuccine with Pancetta
and, 40–41
Peperoncini, Steak with Red Wine,
Olives and, 126–127
Pepper
Chicken Diavolo, 98–99
to crush/grind, 99
Pizza Bread, Rosemary-, 10–11
Spaghetti with Romano Cheese,
54–55
Spareribs with White Wine,

Rosemary and, 142–143

Pepper(s), Sweet

Red, Orechiette with Sausage
and, 48–49

Rice, and Shrimp Soup, 28–29

Roasted, Cod Fillets with,
74–75

Tomato, and Onion Salad with
Basil, Summer, 162–163

Pesto

Black Olive, Potato Gnocchi
with, 58–59

Mint, Lamb Steaks with, 132–133

Spaghetti with Grape Tomatoes
and, 56–57

to store, 57, 133

Pilaf, Arborio Rice, with Porcini
Mushrooms, 200–202

Pine Nut(s)

Cookies, Ginger, 212–213

Gorgonzola Pasta with, Marie's,
44–45

Mesclun Salad with Ricotta and,
160–161

Pesto, Mint, Lamb Steaks with,
132–133

Pizza Bread, Rosemary-Pepper,
10–11

Polenta

with Cheese and Walnuts,
62–63

lump-free, 63

with Salami Sauce, Zia Pia's,
64–65

Porcini Mushrooms, Arborio Rice
Pilaf with, 200–202

Pork

Chops Braised with Marsala,
136–137

Chops with White Wine
Tomato Sauce, 138–139

Spareribs with White Wine,
Rosemary, and Black Pepper,
142–143

See also Pancetta; Prosciutto;
Sausage(s) Potato(es)

Baked, with Romano Cheese,
198–199

Cod Fillets with Roasted Sweet
Peppers and (variation),
74–75

Green Beans and Zucchini with,

184–185

Little New, with Lemon Zest,
196–197

Salad, Italian-Style, 164–165

Turkey Breast, Roast, with
Marjoram, Sage and, 118–119

See also Gnocchi, Potato

Pot Roast with Red Wine, Italian
Style, 130

Prosciutto

as antipasti, 17

and Cannellini Bean Soup, 20–21

for flavoring soups, 27

Provolone, Beef Patties with Red
Wine and, 122–123

Puree of Spinach and Lentil Soup,
26–27

Puttanesca, Risotto (variation),
69–70

R

Radicchio, Green Beans with,
182–183

Red Peppers, Sweet, Orechiette

with Sausage and, 48–49

Red Sauce, Meatballs in,
Old-Fashioned, 128–129

Red Wine

Beef Patties with Provolone and,
122–123

Broccoli with Black Olives and,
176–177

Peaches in, with Almonds,
218–219

Pot Roast with, Italian Style, 130

Ragù, Mini-Rigatoni with, 50–51

Steak, Grilled, Tuscan-Style,
124–125

Rice

Pilaf, Arborio, with Porcini
Mushrooms, 200–202

Salad with Green Dressing,
166–167

Sweet Pepper, and Shrimp Soup,
28–29

See also Risotto

Ricotta

in Espresso Cream, 208–209

fresh, to drain, 209

Fresh, with Fruit, 220–221

Mesclun Salad with Pine Nuts
and, 160–161

Rigatoni, Mini-, with Red Wine
Ragù, 50–51

Risotto

Garlic, Golden, and Cabbage,
66–67

Puttanesca (variation), 69–70

with Tuna and Tomatoes, Quick,
68–69

Romano Cheese

pecorino, about, 55

Peppery Spaghetti with, 54–55

Potatoes, Baked, with,
198–199

Roman Swordfish, 88–89

Rosemary

Chicken with, Sauce, 114–115

Lamb Stew with Garlic,
Tomatoes, and, 134–135

Pepper Pizza Bread, 10–11

Spareribs with White Wine,
Black Pepper, and, 142–143

Tomato Cream, Spaghetti with,
52–53

S

Sage

Chicken Breasts with Pancetta
and, 108–109

Potato Gnocchi with Butter,
Tomato and, 60–61

Turkey Breast, Roast, with
Potatoes, Marjoram and,
118–119

Salad(s), 151–169

Arugula and Basil, 152–153

Arugula, Blood Orange, and
Fennel, 154–155

Beet, Shredded, and
Gorgonzola, 156–157

Carrot (variation), 179

Cauliflower, Tossed,
158–159

Green, with Beet Salad
(variation), 157

Mesclun, with Ricotta and Pine
Nuts, 160–161

Pepper, Sweet, Tomato, and
Onion, with Basil, Summer,
162–163

Potato, Italian-Style, 164–165

Rice, with Green Dressing, 166–167

Seafood, with Mint and Scallion, 168–169

Salami
as antipasti, 17
in Chicken Valdostana, 110–111
Sauce, Zia Pia's, Polenta with, 64–65

Sauce(s)
Lemon and Egg, Chicken Breasts in, 100–101
Ragù, canned tomatoes for, 51
Ragù, Red Wine, Mini-Rigatoni with, 50–51
Red, Meatballs in, Old-Fashioned, 128–129
Salami, Zia Pia's, Polenta with, 64–65
White Wine Tomato, Pork Chops with, 138–139
See also Cream; Pesto

Sausage(s)
with Cannellini Beans and

Tomatoes, 140–141
in Meatballs in Red Sauce, Old-Fashioned, 128–129
Orechiette with Sweet Red Peppers and, 48–49

Scallion, Seafood Salad with Mint and, 168–169

Scallops, Sea
Oven-Roasted, with Capers and White Wine, 80–81
Seafood Salad with Mint and Scallion, 168–169

Seafood
Salad with Mint and Scallion, 168–169
See also Fish; Shellfish

Shellfish
Clams, Steamed, with Garlic and Olive Oil, 72–73
Mussels Steamed with Tomatoes and Vegetables, 78–79
Salad, Seafood, with Mint and Scallion, 168–169
Scallops, Sea, Oven-Roasted, with Capers and White

Wine, 80–81
See also Shrimp

Shrimp
with Anchovy Butter, 82–83
to dry, 85
with Garlic, Onion, and Tomato, 84–85
with Lemon and Garlic, 12–13
Rice, and Sweet Pepper Soup, 28–29
Seafood Salad with Mint and Scallion, 168–169

Sole with Parmesan Glaze, 86–87

Soup(s), 18–33
Cannellini Bean and Prosciutto, 20–21
Chickpea and Escarole, 18–19
Fontina and Bread, 22–23
Green Beans and Greens, 24–25
Lentil and Spinach, Puree of, 26–27
prosciutto as flavoring, 27
Rice, Sweet Pepper, and Shrimp, 28–29
Tomato, Basil, and Bread, 30–31
Tortellini en Brodo, 32–33

Spaghetti

    with Grape Tomatoes and Pesto, 56–57

    with Romano Cheese, Peppery, 54–55

    with Rosemary Tomato Cream, 52–53

Spareribs with White Wine, Rosemary, and Black Pepper, 142–143

Spinach

    Baked, with Garlic Bread Crumbs, 192–193

    and Lentil Soup, Puree of, 26–27

    with Mascarpone, 190–191

    Risotto, and Golden Garlic (variation), 67

Squash, Summer, Grilled, with Parsley and Oregano, 194–195

Steak(s)

    Grilled, Tuscan-Style, 124–125

    Lamb, with Mint Pesto, 132–133

    with Red Wine, Olives, and Peperoncini, 126–127

Stew, Lamb, with Garlic, Tomatoes,

and Rosemary, 134–135

Strawberries, Balsamic Vinegar-Glazed, 222–223

Summer Squash, Grilled, with Parsley and Oregano, 194–195

Swordfish, Roman, 88–89

T

Toasts. *See* Bruschetta

Tomato(es)

    Bass, Sautéed, with Fresh Basil and, 92–94

    canned, for Ragù, 51

    Chicken Cacciatore, 96–97

    Chicken Legs, Roast, with Balsamic Vinegar and, 112–113

    Cream, Rosemary, Spaghetti with, 52–53

    Eggplant with Red Onion and, 180–181

    Garlic, and Onion, Shrimp with, 84–85

    Grape, Spaghetti with Pesto

and, 56–57

    Lamb Stew with Garlic, Rosemary, and, 134–135

    multicolor, 94

    Mussels Steamed with Vegetables and, 78–79

    to peel and seed, 93

    Potato Gnocchi, with Butter, Sage and, 60–61

    in Pot Roast with Red Wine, Italian-Style, 130–131

    Red Sauce, Meatballs in, Old-Fashioned, 128–129

    Risotto, Quick, with Tuna and, 68–69

    Sausages with Cannellini Beans and, 142–143

    Soup, Basil, Bread and, 30–31

    Sweet Pepper, and Onion Salad with Basil, Summer, 162–163

    White Wine Sauce, Pork Chops with, 138–139

Tortellini en Brodo, 32–33

Tuna

    as antipasti, 17

    packed in olive oil, 69

Risotto, Quick, with Tomatoes
and, 68–69
Sautéed, with Crisp Garlic and
Black Olives, 90–91
Turkey
Breast, Roast, with Potatoes,
Marjoram, and Sage, 118–119
Piccata with Mozzarella,
116–117
Tuscan-Style Steak, Grilled,
124–125

V

Veal
Chops with Hazelnuts and
Lemon Cream, 144–145

Scallopini with Lemon, Garlic,
and Bay, 146–147
Vegetables
antipasti ideas, 16–17
in Basil and Olive Oil Dip, 4–5
Mussels Steamed with
Tomatoes and, 78–79
See also specific vegetables

W

Walnuts
Fettuccine, Fresh, with Sweet
Red Onions and, 38–39
Polenta with Cheese and,
62–63
White Wine

Chicken Fricassea with Capers,
104–105
Sea Scallops, Oven-Roasted,
with Capers and, 80–81
Spareribs with Rosemary, Black
Pepper and, 142–143
Tomato Sauce, Pork Chops with,
138–139
Wine. *See* Marsala; Red Wine;
White Wine

Z

Zucchini
and Green Beans with Potatoes,
184–185
with Lemon, 14–15